Effective Urban Densification

The housing crisis confronts two of North America's contemporary urban challenges: affordability and the need to curtail urban sprawl through densification of existing communities. Advancing a novel formula labelled BAAKFIL, this book introduces a new way of thinking about affordability and revitalization of mature neighbourhoods and communities. Beginning with an exploration of the monoculture of homogenous, average quality suburban housing stock in North America, subsequent chapters explore the serious issue of land cost; infill, zoning and Nimbyism in the context of the mass housing industry. Then, bridging the gap between theory and practice, the author introduces a theoretical design approach (BAAKFIL) as a practical formula for adding affordable residential units in established single family neighbourhoods while respecting their defining features. The final chapters evaluate the efficacy of BAAKFIL as a conceptual model by exploring various 'test bed' sites where the framework is applied. This book will be a valuable resource for practicing architects in the housing domain, as well as for planners working in municipalities. It will also appeal to advanced undergraduate and postgraduate students of urban design and architecture.

Barry Johns is a Canadian Architect who began his career with Arthur Erickson in Vancouver, British Columbia. He is a former Chancellor of the College of Fellows, Royal Architectural Institute of Canada and an Honorary Fellow of the American Institute of Architects. His award-winning design practice in Edmonton, Alberta was founded in 1981.

"This book offers valuable ideas and practices to support contemporary residential sustainable planning challenges: affordability and lowering carbon footprint. Barry's vast professional experience is instrumental in translating theories into practice. It is an excellent tool for rethinking suburban communities and inner city neighbourhoods."

Avi Friedman, McGill University,
Montreal, Canada

"Finally, a contribution to the Discipline of Design that offers a specific, scalable model for urban densification. Barry Johns shares with us his deep understanding of the socio-economics of affordable housing and offers a clear path toward multigenerational adaptability and organic community growth."

Brenda Webster Tweel, Stantec,
Toronto, Canada

"BAAKFIL offers a practical and beautiful architectural blueprint. The business model offers an innovative approach to affordability throughout urban and suburban communities. Barry Johns contributes a fresh, hopeful missing middle pathway – a much needed solution to our housing affordability crisis."

Cherise Burda, Toronto Metropolitan University,
Toronto, Canada

Effective Urban Densification

A Guide for Professionals and the Housing Industry

Barry Johns

Routledge
Taylor & Francis Group

NEW YORK AND LONDON

Designed cover image: Jim Dobie

First published 2025
by Routledge
605 Third Avenue, New York, NY 10158

and by Routledge
4 Park Square, Milton Park, Abingdon, Oxon, OX14 4RN

Routledge is an imprint of the Taylor & Francis Group, an informa business

Library of Congress Cataloging-in-Publication Data
A catalog record for this title has been requested

ISBN: 9781032540252 (hbk)
ISBN: 9781032540269 (pbk)
ISBN: 9781003414803 (ebk)

DOI: 10.4324/9781003414803

Typeset in Avenir
by codeMantra

To my children, Melanie, Krista and Graeme, and to my entire family for your love and support.

You lift my spirits.

To my beloved Margo especially, who is always there for me, completely.

Thank you for everything.

This is for you.

Contents

Foreword

I have known Barry Johns for over thirty-five years. Most of that time was by reputation, as one of Edmonton's leading architects. As a registered architect myself, as well as a professor at the University of Calgary's School of Architecture, Planning and Landscape, I admired from afar Barry's prolific portfolio of built work and respected his achievement of a Governor General's Award in Architecture in 1992, our profession's highest recognition for built projects. However, it wasn't until about ten years ago that I got to know Barry personally, when we served together as board members of the Royal Architectural Institute of Canada. In those meetings, Barry was consistently outspoken and always ready to lead with his heart, challenging his fellow board members to remember our profession's obligation to build vibrant, sustainable places that improve the quality of life for all citizens. This passionate commitment to society was a side of Barry I hadn't seen before and, when I became Dean of the school and founded our Doctor of Design (DDes) program in 2019, Barry was at the top of the list of people I thought would be a good candidate for the degree. Fortunately for all of us, Barry was intrigued by the opportunity.

The DDes is a new breed of doctoral degree, and the first of its kind in Canada. Instead of training young academics for a university career, the DDes is an opportunity for experienced architects, planners, and landscape architects to delve deep into their area of expertise and create an innovation that can radically transform their practice and the world. Barry was a member of our inaugural cohort, graduating in 2023. I was honoured to be his supervisor and watch the ideas described in this book take shape.

I will not soon forget the application letter Barry submitted for entry into the program. He was angry and frustrated about the way the established communities of Edmonton (and by extension most other car-centric North American cities) are being gentrified. Modest post-war single family houses on large lots are rapidly being replaced by very large single family houses on those same lots. At best the property might be split in two, but even then, the new houses are oversized, eating up most of the back and front yards. The result is no appreciable increase in density, a massive decrease in affordability, and a significant change in the nature of the community. At that time, Barry thought he had the beginnings of an architectural solution but felt that there was a wall of status quo thinking that would stop it from ever being realized.

In my experience as an architectural entrepreneur, being mad and frustrated at a situation you think you can fix is a good start but on its own doesn't really accomplish much in the way of instigating actual real change. In fact, I believe it is one of the biggest limiting factors our professions face. Outdated models of practice, based on nineteenth-century norms, train architects, planners, and landscape architects to believe that we need to wait for an enlightened client to come along who has a similar vision that allows us to fully exercise our skills and develop an innovative solution. But that isn't usually how innovation works. As Henry Ford reportedly said, "If I asked people what they wanted they would have said a faster horse". True innovation often requires a disruptive change that can't wait for permission from a client. It is driven by a deep belief in a better future combined with a crystal-clear strategy for how to bring that innovation into reality. It requires designers to step outside of their comfort zone and design the context, often financial and operational, in which their idea can flourish.

That is the promise of the DDes program. It is the challenge Barry undertook in his doctoral research, and the result is what he so eloquently describes in this book.

Barry has gone beyond the traditional realm of architectural design to create a new business model, called BAAKFIL, that enables him, and other architects, to do the kind of infill housing he believes in. BAAKFIL empowers homeowners to unlock some of the value in their large lot properties and increase the number and affordability of new dwelling units in established communities without disrupting their appealing low-scale character. This business model creates the context in which Barry's vision of beautifully sensitive and sustainable backyard infill housing projects can become a reality.

Like most great innovations, BAAKFIL is based on a simple idea. Until now, large lot homeowners had only two options—remain living on an expensive piece of land or sell the entire property to a developer to release that equity and move to a different neighbourhood. BAAKFIL provides a third, blended option, that fractionalizes the backyard into a series of smaller lots that can be sold by the homeowner for redevelopment while still retaining ownership of the existing house. The homeowner wins by releasing some of the equity that was locked into the large lot and has the option of continuing to live in their home. The developer and new homebuyers win through a lower land cost for their new home which helps make them more affordable. Finally, the community benefits by increasing density in a gentle way that does not disrupt the original single family streetscape. The fractionalization of products and services (think timeshare condos, co-working spaces, tool rental cooperatives, Uber, and Airbnb) is a well-established innovation strategy. Barry's creative insight is to translate this business idea into an architectural context through a fractionalized backyard strategy that has the potential to revolutionize the way in which established communities are redeveloped.

In this book, Barry outlines the context of the North American, specifically Canadian, single family housing industry and the role homeowners, financial institutions, builders, and developers play in the evolving future of single family post-war neighbourhoods. He describes how the current redevelopment model favors McMansion-style housing and introduces the BAAKFIL model as a subtle disruption of the status quo. Fortunately, he also demonstrates his architectural design prowess with a demonstration project that shows the kind of high-quality residential environment BAAKFIL could deliver.

The current housing affordability crisis adds additional significance to BAAKFIL. Governments at all levels are re-evaluating density regulations and incenting new types of housing. While some may argue that the BAAKFIL approach may not be sufficiently aggressive because of its gentle approach to densification, I believe it can play an important role in a broader suite of densification options for a city. Not all neighbourhoods are well-suited for row housing and multi-level apartment-style housing. Not all homeowners want that radical a shift in where and how they live. In these cases, BAAKFIL provides an important half-step option that retains the existing single family housing stock and the character of the neighbourhood while still increasing density three or four-fold with affordable housing stock.

This book is important to architects and other city builders on two levels. For those with an interest in the business and the art of housing, it offers a blueprint for a different way of approaching established community redevelopment. For venturous design practitioners, young and old, who are fed up with waiting for enlightened clients to change the world, this book is also a prime example of how architects can apply their design-thinking skills to the creation of an innovative practice model that enables them to pursue their beliefs and passions in new ways.

Barry, who through this most recent DDes experience together I now consider a friend, has accomplished something quite extraordinary in this book. BAAKFIL points towards a new way of thinking for our cities and for the design professions responsible for creating them.

John Brown, PhD, Architect

Acknowledgements

The research and development of this publication would not be possible without the commitment of my Supervisory Committee at the University of Calgary. Thanks to my supervisor and Dean, Dr. John Brown and my committee members Associate Professor Marc Boutin and Professor Dr. Joseli Macedo for their dedication and wisdom. I credit John in particular for his deep commitment to my research and for inventing the term 'fractionalization of land' as it refers to my BAAKFIL business model. I use this term sparingly and with attribution since it is not my own, but it is a great descriptor. I also thank Barry Wylant, Director of Graduate Programs and Greg Hart who also supported the work and provided considerable insight.

All photos, illustrations, graphics and drawings are by the author unless otherwise attributed, however, I want to sincerely thank my student team, Bobby Harris and Jessica Williams from Athabasca University for the drone photography and digital renderings for Demonstration Project 1; Dr. Douglas MacLeod, Director of the RAIC Centre for Architecture and MITACS for supporting them. Thanks to my long time consultant, friend and webmaster Chad Oberg for your ongoing loyalty and digital creativity. Thanks to Stephen Ellis and Jeff Pelton at Ellis Associates for the superb BAAKFIL infrastructure model; and to Jim Dobie for the wonderful photography. Many others at the University of Calgary one way or another, helped me along the way, from Jen Taillefer and Miko Lowan Trudeau to my fellow DDes cohort of Michael Donaldson, Teresa Goldstein, Steve McIlvenna, Amy Tsang and Micheal Williamson, now lifelong friends. To my Key Informants especially, I am deeply grateful.

My thanks go to Taylor & Francis Group/Routledge Publishing; Megha Patel and Evie Lonsdale who reviewed my initial book proposal and the editorial board who believed in this publication. To my editors Katherine Schell, Selena Hostetler, Sarah Rae, copyeditor Jane Fieldsend, production editor Alanna Donaldson and the typesetting team of Rajamalar Rathnasekar and codeMantra for steering its final development onto the pages of this book.

Symbols and Abbreviations

AI	Artificial Intelligence
AAA	Alberta Association of Architects
AST	Architect Stakeholder Team
Agri-hood	Integrated agriculture and housing neighborhood
Bare land condo	Plot of land with ground access structures owned by individuals
BJAL	Barry Johns Architecture Limited
BMO	Bank of Montreal
CERB	Canadian Emergency Response Benefit
Charrette	(Fr.) Workshop for concerted (design) problem solving
CMHC	Central Mortgage and Housing Corporation
CoP	Community of Practice
DDes	Doctor of Design
Devco	Development company
DP	Down payment
DSR	Design Science Research
ERV	Energy recovery ventilator
Fractionalization	Appropriation/sale of a land parcel to another party within a titled lot
FRAIC	Fellow Royal Architectural Institute of Canada
(Hon)FAIA	Honorary Fellow American Institute of Architects
GST	Goods and Services Tax
HRV	Heat Recovery Ventilator
ICF	Insulated concrete forms
IRISS	Institutional Research Information Services Solution/Research Ethics Board
KI	Key Informants
KI*	Key Informants (non IRISS)
LEED AP	Leadership in Energy and Environmental Design Accredited Professional
LRT	Light rail transit
Missing Middle	Multi-unit housing including row housing, triplex and fourplex, stacked row housing, courtyard housing and walk up apartments
MLS	Multiple Listing Service
NAIT	Northern Alberta Institute of Technology
NIMBY	Not In My Backyard
NORC	Naturally occurring retirement community
Parti	(Fr.) General scheme of an architectural design

P+W	Perkins & Will
RAIC	Royal Architectural Institute of Canada
RCA	Royal Canadian Academy of Arts
SIPS	Structural insulated panel systems
UDI	Urban Development Institute
UPC	Urban Planning Committee
WOONERF	Living street with shared space, traffic calming and low speed limits
Yield Street	Narrow carriageway traffic calmed street, forcing yield to oncoming vehicles

Chapter 1

Introduction

1.1 Preface

Housing densification is still a modest movement in most of Canada. While the housing crisis escalated during Covid-19, it has been ongoing for some time, with affordability increasingly at issue. Many cities are challenged by housing policies still largely driven by exclusionary single family zoning. New paradigms introduced over the past 15 years, such as infill for mature urban neighbourhoods, intended to increase density, reduce sprawl and its costly infrastructure yield unintended consequences. Quickly conceived, such policies often struggle for acceptance at the local level.

Here, the house building industry applies *suburban* design standards, ignoring context and place. Infill usually begins with demolition of serviceable housing stock and development of oversized and much more expensive speculative development on a lot; negating original densification policy objectives to 'fill in' the open space gaps in neighbourhoods or to replace dilapidated housing with more density. The reality of neighbourhood disruption, as a result, creates fear and distrust. Infill policy is thus often opposed within mature neighbourhoods where new product is seen as disrespectful and financially out of reach for many wishing to move into these more compact, walkable urban settings with less reliance on the automobile.

Within the context of densification, urban design and resilient cities, the influence of the suburban, single family house business model remains omnipresent. Innovation within this system is all the more elusive when zoning bylaws restrict medium density housing typologies, often referred to as the 'missing middle' and mixed use. As a result, choice, variety, flexibility and affordability is limited. This is a daunting challenge while trying to adapt to the shifting demographics of the aging baby-boomer population and smaller households.

Since Covid-19, a surge of interest rate hikes and inflation has yielded an even more acute crisis in housing availability and affordability in Canada and across much of North America. Societal expectations for adequate shelter that were not being met earlier, now see higher income earners such as teachers, nurses and other professionals unable to afford to purchase a house.

Governments at every level claim the solution is to simplistically increase the housing supply, at all costs. Despite history showing that dramatic increases in supply and demand generally result in increased prices; supply chain disruptions (beginning with Covid-19), alongside geopolitical strife around the world, has further induced an even larger global inflationary pattern. Such uncertainty raises even more questions about the efficacy of this *increase supply only* strategy.

Three years of research into the housing crisis exposes the work of many municipalities that are finally planning or implementing zoning reform with much needed removal of barriers to encourage growth and increased density in existing neighbourhoods. Unfortunately, current events are now driving decisions based on expediency, i.e. providing flexible zoning that removes barriers to the *developer* rather than increasing flexibility for responsible neighbourhood densification and sustainable, resilient city building.

The densification agenda today requires respect for context and neighbourhood character, encouraging needed typologies such as multigenerational living and aging in community. The housing emergency is now changing that agenda to just putting more familiar product to market as soon as possible. Policy aimed at addressing the crisis, in other words, is prioritizing the industry itself at the expense of responsible planning and design, neighbourhood self-determination and community resiliency.

This book introduces BAAKFIL©, a new paradigm to address the housing crisis. Its urban context is rooted in the mature neighbourhoods of prairie cities, specifically Edmonton, Alberta. Here, predominant single family detached housing and back alley service lanes dating from the 1950s represent and symbolize the ubiquitous post-war suburban housing ideal found throughout North America.

BAAKFIL is a scalable solution across Canada and indeed, much of the North American urban spectrum. Single family zoning is today being increasingly superseded—yielding a timely area of study; yet affordability remains the major housing issue of our time. As an architectural practice-based solution that addresses this issue, BAAKFIL includes a new business model and a design tool-kit to illustrate how this model can be applied.

The intersection of the housing question, city building and the environment today is a complex study. The pragmatic commodification of the mass housing industry as product driven, like a smart phone, creates a monoculture that traditionally denies the architect a meaningful role in developing new typologies or innovative approaches to the crisis we face. Why cannot architecture take its rightful place in addressing these issues? Ironically, Frank Lloyd Wright said it clearly when he decried the state of the North American city (Wright, 1936, in Pfeiffer, 2011, p. 22):

Architecture must now construct anew the whole social pattern of our time as a new order of the human spirit.

BAAKFIL is one architect's attempt to demonstrate an unusual but practical approach to affordability—that of eliminating land cost to the developer/builder and mitigating land cost to the consumer. Urbanistically, BAAKFIL importantly promotes preservation and gentle densification of existing mature neighbourhoods, in response to socio-cultural needs, changing demographics, sustainable revitalization and community acceptance.

The business model uses equity leveraging to unlock the potential of underutilized land; where an owner partners with a developer by putting up backyard space for development while retaining tenure in the original house and property. The developer builds new housing without purchasing or financing land. Land cost is removed from the project proforma, dramatically reducing development costs and instantly increasing affordability to the consumer.

The BAAKFIL Design Tool-kit gives agency to the landowner (who continues to live in place and is not displaced) in promoting the design of sustainable, respectful architecture, responsive to neighbourhood context.

Broader conclusions are drawn in this book around density, the micro-community and sustainable, resilient cities. BAAKFIL improves the ecology of urban neighbourhoods by preserving streetscapes and advocating the revitalization of city alleys.

BAAKFIL is an acronym for Back Alley Advantage, Kinship, Family & Integrated Living. It is a densification model that supports the preservation of existing housing and population growth at the same time. BAAKFIL integrates the fractionalization of land—an innovation *within* the housing industry—at societal scale. It positions the architect inside the mass housing question to advocate the big idea of maintaining community structures that organically respond to demographics and change, the social pattern of our time. As Jane Jacobs so eloquently championed the values of community engagement (Jacobs, 1961, p. 238):

> *Cities have the capability of providing something for everybody; only because, and only when, they are created by everybody.*

With gentle densification of mature neighbourhoods over time, BAAKFIL increases affordability with respect to and redeeming socio-cultural value.

Architects, builders, designers, academics and students can consider the ideas and principles of BAAKFIL, using this book as a resource to influence and promote respectful housing densification and affordability initiatives within one's own regional context.

1.2 Book Structure

This publication is comprised of seven chapters and author's notes. The format is sequential to define the problem and its context, then explore the evolution, development and evaluation of BAAKFIL along a continuum. Each chapter can be subsequently referenced on its own, according to the reader's particular interest.

Chapter 1 Introduction establishes reasons for the research and encapsulates the body of work in the book. It describes a new paradigm for respectful densification of mature neighbourhoods in the city with a specific approach to The City of Edmonton, Alberta, Canada. This is achieved through the development of a practice-based business model and an architectural design tool-kit to illustrate how the model can be deployed. A narrative entitled 'Reflections of Home' is the start point of this journey; a retrospective that probes the big idea of 'house as home' during a lifetime living in myriad housing typologies across Canada.

Chapter 2 The Problem explores the context and development of the research agenda. It analyses 'the housing question' through precedent projects that describe relevant career experience and qualifications that establish keen interest in the issues to be addressed. The context of the mass housing industry and the over-riding issues within it are examined. The methodology of design science research (DSR) is introduced as integral to the findings. The value of this research methodology using subject matter Key Informants (KI) and one's own community of practice (CoP) is further described to establish the criteria for what becomes the development of the creative project called BAAKFIL.

Chapter 3 BAAKFIL is the description of the creative project. This chapter introduces the concept through personal experience, design, reflection and research input from initial key informant interviews.

Chapter 4 BAAKFIL Business Model describes the unique characteristics of the business model: to eliminate land cost. The business model is expanded into a separate narrative that presents the research input in detail from the perspective of each of the major protagonists in conversation about the housing question: the banker, the developer, the landowner and the consumer.

Chapter 5 BAAKFIL Design Tool-kit is separately formatted within the body of this book, so it stands alone as a primer about the conceptual BAAKFIL design strategies. It includes design and technical principles to describe a generic (yet still allows a bespoke) approach to respectful scale and site design that fits within a net zero sustainability agenda.

Chapter 6 Demonstration Projects includes two demonstration projects as proof of concept: one being a compilation of the various characteristics of the business model and design of a BAAKFIL development on a 'pie' lot shaped site in The City of Edmonton; the other a more pragmatic rental project on a corner lot in the city. Both projects explore the potential of the business model and bring into focus a practical, achievable idea to address the housing crisis of attainability, affordability, agency for landowners, respectful densification and city making. As further proof of concept, this chapter includes an evaluation resulting from a second round of key informant interviews. Finally, a Design Fiction narrative fast forwards five years to explore BAAKFIL on the site of one of the demonstration projects, through the eyes of a consumer.

Chapter 7 Conclusion processes the design science research methodology through personal reflection about the learnings and how this impacts the author's practice of architecture. It is also an observation of BAAKFIL as a conceptual framework for future-proofing: a measure of its veracity and what might be appropriate to examine next as a research or development initiative.

Author's Notes provides a description of the design science research (DSR) methodology, its high level impact and how it is different from natural science-based research; alongside a survey of the author's professional background and qualifications.

1.3 Narrative: Reflections of Home: Looking Back to the Future

My story begins in Montreal

I was born into a working class family with modest means, but raised with a strong sense of family and community. As I think about this in the context of the Doctor of Design, I realize my life journey has included many cities and almost every type of housing available across Canada. The typologies that enable some of my fondest memories are, however, scarcely available or even permitted in some cities today; due to extraordinarily high land cost, restrictive zoning bylaws, the commodified business model of the single family housing industry and a 'push back' mindset against densification in neighbourhoods and communities. In my professional practice, we find this inhibits creative responses to changing demographics, even to the idea of change itself. This has yielded mediocrity in the cross section of many cities, standardized materials and design control mechanisms, limited choice and rigid regulations that create a serious housing attainability and affordability crisis across the country.

▲ Figure 1.3.1

Infill House, Montreal, PQ

Why does our current legislation preclude our ability to enjoy life as we once did?

My parents met before and married after the war, moving next to both the Johns and Rimmer families on Greene Avenue in Montreal in 1946. The sons, especially, veterans all, maintained deep kinships but never talked about the years between 1939 and 1945, when they were enlisted in the navy and the army at ages 18, 19 and 20—at least not in front of parents, wives and, later, children.

Before the post-war building boom and establishment of the suburban ideal of a single family home, they all lived in superposed flats or 'plexes' as they were known in Montreal; a very common and successful housing typology throughout the city. A very simple concept—attainable and affordable—plexes were mostly three storeys high, connected in rows up to a block in length, tight to the street with gardens at the back. While not very permeable within the block, streets were walkable, with flats distinguished by their often picturesque and totally impractical outdoor stairs or 'stoops', many rather poetically

▼ Figure 1.3.2

'Plex' housing, Greene Avenue, Montreal, PQ

curved. The owner usually lived on the ground floor and rented out the upper two floors to pay the mortgage.

My life began here, in one of these rented flats.

Our extended families on Mother's side either coexisted in the same building or in the neighbourhood. It was a close knit, walkable environs. Our families, who would later disperse to other parts of the city, continued to regularly visit my grandmother and uncles when they moved to a larger plex in Verdun.

Childhood memories abound. My grandmother whose husband passed before I could really remember him, except for his pipe; and two of her five sons who worked nearby and, being single at the time, shared the flat with her. Sunday's were for family dinners and I have a vivid memory of being assaulted upon our arrival by the lingering smell of stale pipe tobacco in the walls of the upper stairwell entrance. My brother and I would be regaled by our talkative Nanny Johns about her intimate knowledge of the Montreal Canadiens, a hockey dynasty at the time. She knew all the players, their 'stats' and had met a few of them personally over the years, so she would entertain us with gossip all night long. We loved it.

One of our other uncles owned a small corner store where you could buy everything, but mostly cigarettes and beer. Being the older brother, it was my job to stock up for the family before our dinners, despite being only nine or ten at the time. In Quebec in the late 1950s, if the money was handed over to you, even kids could pick up those supplies. Why? Because everybody knew who you were. This was a community, built on friendship, trust and neighbourliness.

My uncle lived above their store and he rented the top floor of his plex. Some folks would stay for years. Home ownership had not yet become a coveted phenomenon. My other grandparents on my Mother's side lived nearby and were also hockey fans. This was indeed a religion in Montreal. We loved hating Toronto and the feared Leafs. Grandad Rimmer worked in the famed Montreal Forum on Atwater Street (also permanently smelling of smoke) for 35 years. We got standing room playoff tickets for free.

Grandad was gifted a newly weaned collie by the owner of the Canadiens who raised show dogs on his farm in Sherbrooke. Too old to look after a new pup and with us having moved to Valois, we ended up with a family pet for 12 years. Families and work loyalties were deeply connected. To this day, a picture of 'Sport' is in my wallet.

Learnings: Plex housing typologies are popular in Montreal even today. Parvarash (Parvarash, 2016) writes in her 2016 PhD dissertation at l'Université de Montréal that traditional plex neighbourhoods continue to offer accessible, affordable and flexible housing now sought by people among the 29–45 age group. Creating a strong 'sense of place', affordability is addressed by different forms of ownership while liveable front to back unit layouts enable a variety of uses, change and urban neighbourhood densities that nurture community over the longer term. This was the beginning of 'missing middle', before the term was invented, for me in Montreal.

Figure 1.3.3

Valois Infill house, Montreal, PQ

In Valois, we lived in what is now called an 'infill', doubling the density of the long skinny lot on which the house sat in the rear. Built by the owners who lived at the front, it was rented to the caretaker of my elementary school that we backed onto. The caretaker eventually bought the property, moved to the front and we moved into his former house at the back—20 feet wide and single storey with a crawl space that my Dad, brother and I dug out over three summers to make a partial basement and shop. The house was small, discreet and respectful, with a glass porch that, despite being unheated, was a place for meals, board games and naps during the hot, humid Montreal summers and temperate shoulder seasons.

I would learn the important social significance of porches and verandahs over time—the unheated, neighbourly living room. Later I would spend an entire summer with my girlfriend and future wife (who I met at University but who also lived in Montreal) at EXPO 67, with our youth passports. We would rest, exhausted after each site visit, inside her parents back porch overlooking the garden.

In addition to its proximity to the school, our infill house was within easy walking distance of Valois Park, our home base for summer and winter sports. One winter during Montreal's infamous ice storms when the power was out for days, my brother and I were invited by the caretaker's son (who would later play professional baseball) to join him to set up and use all the equipment in the school gym where power had been quickly restored, but the streets and school were still closed. We spent days there in our private sports centre weathering the storm playing volleyball, climbing ropes, using the mats and springboard. We learned to wish for ice storms as kids.

Learnings: Neighbourhoods evolve during good times and bad. Infill when respectful of its surroundings, in scale with compatible materials or colour, is unthreatening and fits in comfortably and unassumingly, despite the doubling of density on a given lot. Verandahs and porches provide eyes on the street and promote connections or 'neighbourliness' as semi-private space where one can see and be seen by neighbours out for a walk. These rooms, even in a winter city, serve many utilitarian and family functions, in front or backyards. They help build community, one room at a time.

Before leaving home for university in the Maritimes, our family moved to a new subdivision across the bridge that leaves the west island of Montreal. I built a bedroom with used barnboards in the basement so my brother and I no longer had to share a room. My other grandmother was invited to live with us and we were so happy for our parents who could finally afford their first house. Even one of my Mother's brothers and our cousins moved to the same development, each living the dream.

Mom and Dad created an intergenerational home that carried forward the life they once knew on Greene Avenue. But we could no longer take the train like we always did from Valois to downtown and I had to always selfishly jockey for a turn to borrow the family car. Thus was imposed an unwanted inconvenience to daily life. With no stores, parks or recreation areas that we could walk or bike to, few trees, big fences and wide streets, it was clear that driving was suddenly a big deal within this new suburban lifestyle.

I was glad to leave.

Learnings: My parents loved their new life, although they couldn't afford to add the front garage—a fixture on the street. They nevertheless made a big garden in the backyard and Dad had his shop in the basement. There was room for them and for us, Nanny Rimmer and Sport, who by then was aging quickly. It just was not for me. I yearned to be closer to downtown and my summer jobs and missed the things I lost—friends, places, organized sports. Unlike the University years to follow, there was little to discover, everything looked the same, there was no sense of being in a place. One of the many things I missed in this monoculture, believe it or not, was a sidewalk.

University involved residence, communal living in flats and soon after, married life in a small apartment. However, a 'rooming house' during my first two years in architecture school in Halifax after three years at Acadia University is worth mentioning. With a private kitchenette, bathroom and 'bed sit'; three self-contained units had been squeezed into the second floor of one house with separate storage for everyone below grade, in a boat hull-shaped structural undercroft. A fourplex in a 1200sf two storey maritime shed roof house! Halifax is a wonderful university city with an unfortunate dearth of student housing. So the owner occupied the ground floor and rented these tiny (150sf) micro apartments to students, albeit an unreliable clientele.

Fourplex main and upper floor,
Halifax, NS

Architecture school meant little social time; but the convenience, cost and independence here was perfect. I stayed—in the city centre with everything I needed within easy walking distance including the school—for two years. I left my belongings in a trunk in the undercroft that first summer, when my unit was rented out short term while I was back in Montreal; only to find it had disappeared when I returned for the fall semester. Shared housing can be a bit shady.

Learnings: At the time, I felt little emotion about this place since I lived for the most part in the studio at school, stealing away infrequently to see my future wife who was still at Acadia. Nevertheless, it was likeable, cheap and clean. With an unassuming street presence, I now realize just how clever this was as a missing middle typology; exceedingly simple yet completely customized for the university student cohort, well suited to a housing need in short supply, but in high demand.

Marriage, graduation and early work would find us in two delightful character houses at opposite ends of the country. Converted into duplexes where we lived on the second floor with the owner below us, Moncton provided us with access on our floor to an incredible sun drenched, multi dormer window and cobwebbed attic (that we dreamt of converting into an upper loft) where we discovered a framed and dusty Cornelius Krieghoff painting in a wooden box—a great story on its own.

We moved into a ubiquitous high rise one-bedroom apartment (but with a splendid view of the mountains) when we pulled up stakes and moved to Vancouver; then found another duplex conversion to settle into after we had learned our way around the city. These two

▲ Figure 1.3.5

Duplex, Moncton, NB

old homes doubled their lot density within their existing walls, their street presence unchanged in their single family neighbourhoods. Modest interventions both, they subtly betrayed their multi-tenant occupancy with two little mailboxes beside the front door.

Learnings: Densification has a positive impact on community and neighbourhood relationships when handled respectfully. Duplex conversions are everywhere—some legal while others are technically not. Importantly, many of these wonderful old houses can accommodate more! Moncton with its attic developed could easily have become a gracious triplex. As such these are completely benign typologies. Negative community impacts that people are so fearful of is often a myth when care and respectful design is deployed. Our Moncton rent paid for the owner's house maintenance and utility bills while our Vancouver rent paid for the owner's grad school tuition. They also became friends. The neighbours were great. The street was unchanged.

False Creek townhouse,
Vancouver, BC

We would become some of the first residents of a new co-op housing development in False Creek, Vancouver; living in a three-storey, 14 foot wide townhouse with an upper roof deck and small studio that commanded uninterrupted views to the north shore mountains.

This successful living concept in a city that experienced enormous land value increases in the mid 1970s (and continues unabated today) provided us with awesome new digs in a central location, where we would otherwise not be able to afford to buy. We found ourselves happily ensconced within walking distance of everything we needed, without our car. Even with a young family and a couple of bicycles, with those Saarinen inspired pre-formed fibreglass kid seats, we were wonderfully mobile.

Learnings: Co-op housing is commonplace in cities where land value skyrockets (Smith, 2020). It is a model with many iterations that enable a level of affordability where none might otherwise exist. Popular with residents, the system would never go mainstream with developers. The time and effort required to assemble land for such development could not compete with the profitability of either bare land or multi-storey apartment condominiums. Co-ops remain largely misunderstood and a cultural enigma in some sectors, although interestingly, much of New York City is comprised of co-op housing.

I started my own practice on the Canadian prairie and we moved into a classic Edmonton bungalow in a mature 1960s' neighbourhood ten minutes from downtown. We totally rebuilt its interior, removing one bedroom to create a two-storey central atrium that opened to the basement to let the light in. Here we developed a master bedroom suite instead of a recreation room. We next added a split level wing—a garage under with two sloped ceiling studio bedrooms for our two daughters above. The remaining bedrooms became a separate room for our son, the other opened to the atrium as the family TV room. The children could adapt as they grew older with privacy whenever needed and we had our own space below in the two-story atrium sitting area. We were always connected but could still be separate.

Finally, we added the architect Charles Moore's typical Sea Ranch Condominium 'saddlebag' extensions to make a bigger entry

▲ Figure 1.3.7

Parkview bungalow, Edmonton, Alberta

and kitchen. The house enabled many subtle demographic shifts over time as the children grew from Sesame Street into computers, teenage and the university years. The entire renovation was completed by simply extending the original roofline of this corner lot towards the back alley.

People could not believe that we created an unassuming split level, light filled atrium house with studios above a garage within such a low profile. We wanted to remain authentic to the predominantly single storey bungalow neighbourhood, but we nevertheless nicknamed our place the 'un-bungalow'.

Learnings: This was our old walkable neighbourhood of Parkview—where I first discovered the changes taking place due to poorly conceived bylaw 'amendments'. We sold the house in three days, given the immense popularity, walkability and central neighbourhood location. Within a decade however, it had irreversibly changed.

Many properties along our street, including our own former property, were re-landscaped with rock as a predominant material. Properties were destroyed with 'monster' homes—single family dwellings of up to 5000sf with mature trees sacrificed to make room. These buildings dwarfed their neighbours and were built of the same common materials found in new subdivisions—plastic plank siding, perforated metal soffits and fascias, fake stone, small windows, recycled roof shingles (to make them all 'green') and cheap landscaping.

Then the infill bylaws were introduced (Edmonton, 2009)—with some houses almost as large, three storeys with flat roofs and roof decks overlooking everyone else's backyard. The neighbourhood character dramatically changed—but every new house met the bylaws. I emphasize the importance of respectful development here. Disrespect does not maintain or sustain a community. Neighbours become distant, less welcoming and disconnected.

We spent a decade living in a wonderful 1960s' modern, Unitarian church in the historic neighbourhood of Westmount. It was lovingly restored by us and converted into a rather eccentric place where a big kitchen enabled our now dispersed, grown family to visit and stay and work together preparing meals. It was a courtyard building comprising an architectural studio fully equipped with guest quarters for the children, visiting guests, friends and colleagues.

We became daily eyes on the street in the neighbourhood, with no traffic. As a former church it would be filled with people and traffic engorged streets on weekends, but remain largely empty during the week. We'd walk our dog Piper (a sheltie—aka 'miniature' collie) through the narrow, leafy yield streets, saying hi to the neighbours on their porches or verandahs or tending their front gardens; walking to the office and stopping for supplies at the night market or along the 124 Street commercial and arts corridor. This was an enormous contrast to Parkview. Yet, given this historic neighbourhood with old, turn of the century houses, many properties over time became duplexes like Moncton and Vancouver, some legal others not, while others still are rented to students or house their parents in a multigenerational enclave.

▲ Figure 1.3.8

Unitarian Church, Edmonton, Alberta

Learnings: Even Westmount, as old and gentrified as it has become with its narrow 'yield' streets, mature elms, street parking (most everyone uses their lane facing garages for storage) and successful missing middle examples, is eroding with infill that is completely disrespectful of the historic context. The bylaws define entitlements based on setbacks, floor area ratios and height—all predicated on zoning bylaw principles conceived 70 years ago with new subdivisions. They are not about design quality or maintaining neighbourhood character. It is legal in some cases to remove mature trees. This results in antipathy toward new development, even fear in neighbourhoods when this could legally occur next door. This is the unintended consequence of densification in urban neighbourhoods.

▲ Figure 1.3.9

Townhouses, Edmonton, Alberta (Google Earth)

Today, we split our time between a rebuilt town house and, due to Covid-19, self-isolation at our lake cottage. (We certainly recognize our good fortune to be able to do so.) The townhouse, originally constructed in the 1980s for mature professionals, is part of a condominium complex of 20 units around two courtyards next to a deep, verdant city ravine. It enables us complete freedom to travel as empty nesters where we can just lock up and leave.

We are a small cohort that can self-organize at our own granular level, somewhat like a large family, with flexible bylaws—rules that we can change to guide a rapid response to changing demographics.

Last year a family moved in with two young children, a huge paradigm shift. They have just been granted permission to have a pet. Most others are like us, however, with grandchildren who visit and play on the snow piles in the courtyard. The laughter is welcomed. A couple of units are rented. Two widows in the complex who, with their former husbands were original owners, became long time friends. They are now planning to move in together and rent or sell the other unit. So continues the cycle of life.

During our initial DDes Fall Symposium, discussion around the distinction between the concepts of laws and entitlements, rules and principles was inspiring. This landed on the interesting dichotomy between zoning as a means to enable types of growth (laws) versus the removal of constraints and promotion of self-organization (rules) in communities and neighbourhoods.

Our condominium, built to 1980s' zoning bylaws, is entering new life. Almost every unit is renovated or re-built and we review our bylaws annually. We are enabling organic, physical and social renewal of community—a clear manifestation of successful, shifting 'value sets'.

A zoning free zone.

Learnings: Self-organization at the granular level, works. Zoning may have its place as a macro-level framework (that I might debate) but that is also where it could end. Zoning is neither intended nor appropriate to impose laws at the micro level, i.e. the day to day lives of people and communities. The indelible footprint that zoning leaves behind in cities constipates organic growth and change, as I have discovered. Worse, it militates against creativity and respect for others. This notion is perhaps best illustrated in the popularity and sustainability of what is traditionally called 'Chinatown' (Wikipedia, n.d.) in major cities. Comprised of self-organized organic growth, these cultural urban communities are at once unique, varied, walkable and inclusive.

Argument: Zoning can become the wrong prescription for community need—i.e. the very act of living that precipitates natural pressure for change. Architectural controls in subdivisions are a good example. Legislating colour and materials denies the emergence of eclectic and potentially enchanting variety; such as we see in older pre-war neighbourhoods. Ironically this has negative

consequences in the context of the housing crisis as well.

Single family neighbourhoods in the Yellowbelt (Lorinc, 2019, pp. 28, 29) areas of Toronto (fully 47% of the city's land mass) are recognized as 'precious' and are at this time of writing, totally protected against change of use by law.

The argument to be made, in other words, is that overarching regulations that can go too far, reinforce one cohort's ability to change and live the way they choose as their families grow and shrink, while denying similar rights to others. The Yellowbelt population density is actually dropping—in Canada's largest city. One wonders if renewal here is even possible.

To look at the macro/micro scale together (another outcome of the DDes Fall Symposium) to create more appropriate housing typologies and business models is key to my search for new knowledge.

This essay, thus far, speaks to personal experience at the community/neighbourhood level. To combine this with the macro-level of city making, we look back to where this essay began.

I am proud to stake a claim to Montreal as my city. Here, I learned about being a good neighbour as a youngster and where I would (inadvertently) discover the ideology of 'urban design' and making cities, at an impressionable age.

EXPO 67 (Wikipedia, n.d.) with its stunning planning strategies about people movement and its sense of urban connectivity, created on manmade islands for a mere six-month celebration, was overwhelming. I made the most of it, as has the city itself—finding a permanent place in the hearts and minds of Montréalais and Quebec culture immediately.

With splendid architecture, this 'temporary' urban model showcased pavilions such as Moshe Safdie's Habitat, Arthur Erickson's Katimavik, Buckminster Fuller's geodesic dome and Frei Otto's tensile structures to place architecture in Canada on an international stage.

The new Metro (subway) as an urban *system* (whose mined tailings and excavation materials created the Expo islands in the St Lawrence River in the first place, and in so doing defined the ideal of responsible waste management) yielded a downtown core completely interconnected, it seemed, overnight. Its all-weather underground pedestrian street network, relieved by sunny courtyards open to the sky and street level plazas, myriad shops and services, set an example that was published and revered around the world.

But the true urban design pulse of la Grande Ville de Montréal is found in its more subtle, organic development of communities and inter-racial, multilingual neighbourhood culture. EXPO merely exposed what was already the most cosmopolitan city in North America, to the world.

Depending upon where we lived at any given time, I was never more than a five to 15 minute walk to my schools, parks and playgrounds, pool, rink and what we now call High Street—shops, grocery store, post office, barbershop, soda bar, restaurants and other community services, along Donegani Avenue. We were only a bike ride or a short hitchhike (without my parents knowing) away from the regional shopping centre with its department store, bowling alley, theatre and the lakeshore.

We talk about the 15 minute city today, championed by the current Mayor of Paris as if this is a new idea (Wilshire, 2020; Sisson, 2020). Montreal evolved as a 15 minute city, connected with respect and inclusivity. Many places across the country including many where we have lived, are also 15 minute cities. There were no prescriptive bylaw or lifestyle restrictions at the outset in Montreal. Our only major civic infrastructure system needed was the commuter train to downtown alongside Highway 2+20. This just naturally happened with growth. As naïve as it sounds today, everyone simply got along. My brother and I had English, French and myriad ethnic friends despite going to different schools and the politics of language.

Learnings: The 15 minute city, while not new, is an important catalyst for housing densification and community development. To achieve these macro-level advancements, densification must be accompanied by mixed use opportunities which means flexible bylaws or regulations that eliminate singular use silos, in favour of a more integrated planning structure; not unlike what we never realized we had, when we were children.

These life experiences shape how I know we CAN and DO adapt to change, actually quite easily, from childhood to our senior years, but it is nuanced. We experience this subconsciously. Reflecting on this personal trajectory in the context of *densification responsive to place and demographic change* has re-opened my eyes to the art of the possible.

I plan to go back to this future in my research.

Learnings: I will use life and practice experience to inform my quest to address the housing question.

I will include the 15 minute community as an overarching component to the solution space around densification, place and demographics.

In practice, we are invested in housing typologies but, largely as defined by our clients. We live aspirationally, but we must function as a service business, restricted by time and money to undertake the research needed to make practice more innovative, 'outside the box'.

As architects, we are outliers in the housing market. When offered the chance, we discover a staid, unsympathetic system based on standards, outdated rules and a relatively under-developed industry that still builds with sticks. We finesse our expertise through the minefields of development approvals, compromising budgets, construction vagaries and post-occupancy challenges. Despite some success, we have not changed much.

What is the point of this essay?

As a personal reflection now viewed through the lens of the architect, it helps me focus on the beginning of this journey.

I realize this research process allows me to work within my professional practice without the normal constraints of regulation, client or market-driven decisions.

I am equally curious about what it might be like—as I unknowingly discovered during my naïve younger years as a happy kid, even as a young architect who mostly just enjoyed living where we found ourselves—to not be held hostage to bylaws, or better still, to blow them up.

I now better understand that the answer to a large part of the housing crisis, while manifesting itself in architecture, is NOT about architecture. It is rather more about changing the agenda that influences architecture—land cost, lack of choice, bylaw regulations and the changing demographic of families and households.

Architects have designed extraordinary 'one-off' housing projects for enlightened or liberal clients. But for the general consumer, *innovation*, let alone quality or choice is elusive. Innovation is better enabled by finding ways to reduce or eliminate the negative forces that militate against architecture as a 'cause' to bring forward an environment that enables architecture as a 'solution'.

We are change agents, privileged by holistic education that develops critical thinking skills. We can foresee and encourage the positive aspects of change, without fear.

Within the problem space of the housing question, it is clear this is not the case for the majority of consumers who are fearful of the unknown, subjected to the commodified housing industry that has changed little in 70 years, product driven, without any systemic recognition about bespoke needs, attainability, affordability or demographic change.

This life experience proves important to the research—it informs me about the important value sets inherent to the housing question.

1.4 Preamble

This publication introduces BAAKFIL, a new paradigm to address the housing crisis.

What am I doing?

My objective is to explore practice-based solutions—a new business model and an architectural design tool-kit to illustrate how the model can be applied. I address the housing crisis and densification agenda in mature urban neighbourhoods. My focus is The City of Edmonton; but BAAKFIL as a Pan-Canadian, even North American concept is proposed.

BAAKFIL examines land cost and housing supply to increase affordability. It promotes gentle densification in response to socio-cultural needs and current demographics.

How am I doing this?

I engage the expertise of subject matter experts known as Key Informants through a semi-structured interview process to assist in establishing the problem space and address the research question. I reflect upon precedent projects within and outside my practice to include my Community of Practice (CoP). This creates a fulsome data base. I also reflect upon decisions made while developing a practice-based solution. As the work nears completion, I undergo a second round of interviews with my Key Informants to obtain their feedback on the work. I then reflect on this and finalize the outcomes accordingly.

Why is this important to society?

I offer a new business model and an architectural design tool-kit that impacts affordability and densification. This includes agency to landowners who wish to remain to age in their community and influence the growth and revitalization of their own neighbourhood. This is an overdue proposition for architects to address demographic currency—to take heed of the social patterns of our time—where aging parents and their families increasingly choose to live closer to home or even together, to combat serious affordability issues.

The business model is about equity leveraging and it unlocks the potential of underutilized land; where a landowner partners with a developer by putting up backyard space for development, while retaining tenure in the original house and property. The developer builds new housing without the need to finance land.

Land cost is removed from the project proforma, substantially reducing development costs and instantly increasing affordability. This is a scalable solution across Canada, if not North America.

In addition, a BAAKFIL architectural Design Tool-kit promotes the design of sustainable and respectful architecture, responsive to neighbourhood context.

The social justice perspective of this concept importantly includes respect for growing a neighbourhood without changing it. This is the essence of the resilient city as a living organism, created and nurtured by the people who live in it.

Broader conclusions are drawn about density, the micro-community and sustainable, resilient cities. I also demonstrate that BAAKFIL improves the ecology of urban neighbourhoods by street-scape preservation and advocating the revitalization of city alleys.

BAAKFIL is an acronym for Back Alley Advantage, Kinship, Family & Integrated Living. It is a densification model that supports the preservation of existing housing and population growth at the same time.

Background

At the outset, I fold the crisis of housing affordability into a broader topic that I refer to as 'the housing question'. This is such a vast subject that exposes, among other things, the complicated intersection between *design* and people of all cultures.

The house building industry in North America remains deeply connected to the post World War II building boom that saw the rise of the single family house, suburbia and geographic sprawl. The industry is a major economic driver, yet it remains a relatively unskilled labour-oriented system, compared to the global context of advanced technology and digitization. It continues to yield a monoculture with lack of choice, ignoring changing demographics to smaller households and multigenerational families, while devouring green space and changing established neighbourhoods through densification, often creating fear and antipathy. These *product driven* outcomes are by definition unable to create design-oriented or sustainable solutions to meet bespoke socio-cultural needs and climate resiliency; or commit to basic criteria as proper site and plan organization to capture sunlight and views.

This status quo marketplace is now in a major crisis of attainability and affordability, with dramatic increases over the last generation to the cost of land and infrastructure services.

Covid-19, higher interest rates and inflation merely exacerbate this fundamental problem.

Pivot

My original objective set out to broadly derive flexible, future net zero, missing middle housing typologies for urban neighbourhoods that respond to the specifics of site, climate and culture—and above all—affordability. The housing research question uses the above preamble to frame this *desire path* to focus on a specific, limited scope—*affordability, densification and respect for place*.

The discovery that land cost is the biggest barrier to affordability changes everything. Solving that wicked problem enables virtually everything else around the research objective to fall into place.

Land cost removal and land cost mitigation in the quest for affordability, becomes the essence of this entire publication and what evolves into the BAAKFIL paradigm.

This book posits in other words, a realistic pathway for affordability, innovation and public acceptance, *within* an established housing industry not normally so disposed.

References

Edmonton, C. o. (2009). City of Edmonton. www.edmonton.ca/city_government/urban_planning_and_design/residential-infill-guidelines.aspx

Jacobs, J. (1961). *The Death and Life of Great American Cities*. New York: Vintage Books, Random House Publishing.

Lorinc, J. (2019). The stability trap. In A. Bozikovic (Ed.), *House divided*. Toronto: Coach House Books.

Parvarash, P. (2016). *Montreal's superposed flats_the influence of architecture on…sense of place…Verdun Borough*. PhD Thesis, Université du Québec à Montréal, Montreal. www.archipel.uqam.ca/9446/1/D3199.pdf

Pfeiffer, B. B. (2011). *Frank Lloyd Wright: On architecture, nature and the human spirit*. Petaluma, CA: Pomegranate Communications.

Sisson, P. (2020, December 3). City monitor. https://citymonitor.ai/environment/what-is-a-15-minute-city

Smith, L. (2020, September 2). Investopedia. www.investopedia.com/articles/pf/08/housingco-op.asp

Wikipedia. (n.d.). EXPO 67. https://en.wikipedia.org/wiki/Expo_67

Wikipedia. (n.d.). www.en.wikipedia.org https://en.wikipedia.org/wiki/Chinatown

Wilshire, K. (2020, February 7). *The Guardian*. www.theguardian.com/world/2020/feb/07/paris-mayor-unveils-15-minute-city-plan-in-re-election-campaign

Chapter 2

The Problem

2.1 Precedent Projects

A Canadian Architect based in Edmonton, Alberta, I am currently an independent design consultant, instructor and mentor. Retired from traditional practice after 40 years; I am fortunate to leave behind a legacy of unique, award winning projects.

This chapter connects relevant projects in the history of my practice to the housing question. Specifically, these are housing

▼ Figure 2.1.1

Reflection Road Map

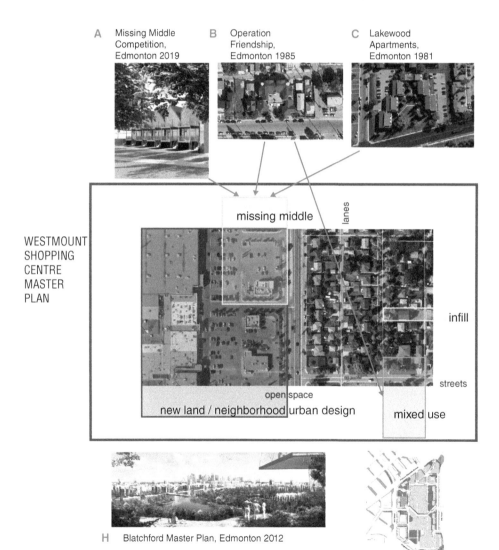

A Missing Middle Competition, Edmonton 2019

B Operation Friendship, Edmonton 1985

C Lakewood Apartments, Edmonton 1981

WESTMOUNT SHOPPING CENTRE MASTER PLAN

missing middle

lanes

infill

streets

open space

new land / neighborhood urban design

mixed use

H Blatchford Master Plan, Edmonton 2012

I Kingsway Master Plan, Edmonton 2013

  DOI: 10.4324/9781003414803-2 CHAPTER 2 The Problem

projects that relate to community and involve many stakeholders. As one finds everywhere, such groups in The City of Edmonton include community leagues and interest groups involved in zoning bylaw reform, the Urban Planning Committee (UPC), officials connected with the new City Plan and membership by invitation with the Architects Stakeholder Team (AST) for The City of Edmonton; all describe a diverse cohort. In addition, numerous other consultations include sub-committees comprising planners,

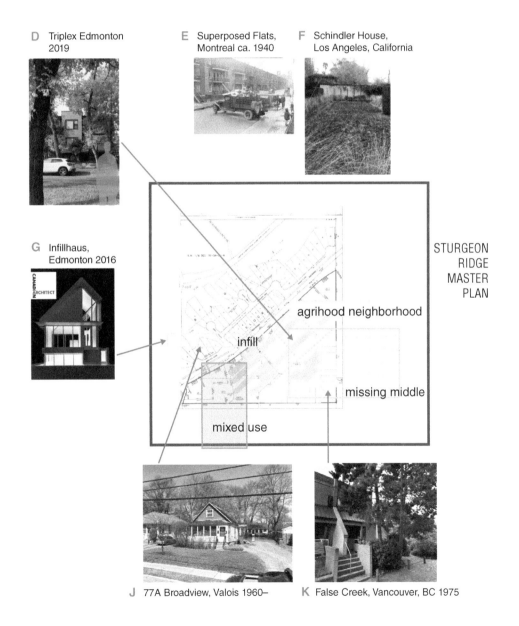

D Triplex Edmonton
   2019

E Superposed Flats,
   Montreal ca. 1940

F Schindler House,
   Los Angeles, California

G Infillhaus,
   Edmonton 2016

STURGEON
RIDGE
MASTER
PLAN

agrihood neighborhood

infill

missing middle

mixed use

J 77A Broadview, Valois 1960–

K False Creek, Vancouver, BC 1975

real estate department representatives, the Edmonton Innovative Housing Lab, Urban Development Institute (UDI) and members of City Council.

Figure 2.1.1 introduces precedent projects by the practice or by others that inform the research objective, from a problem setting and solution setting context. The diagram includes two masterplan proposals for the redevelopment of Westmount, the oldest shopping mall in Edmonton and a new Agri-hood housing community on an organic farm on the outskirts of the city. Both sites are different, yet ask questions about best fit housing typologies and how they can be leveraged within the context of city making. The shopping mall site advocates zero land cost for future housing and mixed use development to stimulate the market while new density allowances in Sturgeon County allow the Agri-hood project to combine with smaller lot sizes (compared to the large acreage properties in the area) to bring land value to more affordable levels, stimulate the market and increase the tax base.

These two projects set the framework for the following precedent projects:

A The 2019 Edmonton Missing Middle Competition entry is a 21-unit bare land condominium with mixed use, multigenerational flexible layouts, lane sidewalks and lane addresses. The competition is based on maximizing density in a mature neighbourhood, promoting the missing middle. The majority of entrants include densities equal to or beyond that contained in the new City Plan up to 105 units/ha. (City of Edmonton, 2020). The City of Edmonton proposes to sell the land at $1.7m and each proponent is obligated to carry this amount in a required cost estimate and project proforma. A majority of the schemes include underground parking, pushing sales prices beyond the absorption limit of the neighbourhood and the project does not proceed. The competition is interpreted by proponents from outside Edmonton as an exercise in celebrating the idea of maximizing density; without regard for community concerns. My practice works with a developer familiar with the neighbourhood and we determine a bare land condominium (ground-oriented access) without underground parking is best and in keeping with the neighbourhood. The land component at $81,000/unit, however, forces the project into financial jeopardy from the outset, given the smaller number of units that are designed to fit comfortably on the site. Our project is not shortlisted.

B Operation Friendship is award winning social services housing to make a small community for the brain damaged alcoholic in the inner city. Mixed uses include 40 rooming house units, a drop-in centre, medical and social services with on-site counselling and administration. A self-effacing and respectful parti, it blends into its neighbourhood to be instantly welcoming and familiar to its abnormal

Missing Middle Competition,
Edmonton, Alberta 2019

clientele. This project is about place. With porches, decks, dormer windows, picket fences and verandahs that echo the neighbourhood, its integration with the inner city context make this project hard to find without knowing its address. As a provincial government project, it is completed outside of the Zoning Bylaws.

C Lakewood Apartments are competition winning, low cost rental, split level units, each with through ventilation and unique 'skip stop' access (one corridor for three floors); a planning device pioneered by LeCorbusier in the Unité D'Habitation projects in Marseille and elsewhere in Europe. All living spaces face a private, central courtyard screened from the street by a large berm and garden. This project is an early reminder of the value of scale and courtyard clustering for sunshine, privacy and safety. The lower levels of the project are partially let into the ground and create a quiet and intimate micro-community. Privacy in this project is provided by the street berm constructed from the foundation excavation material while parking is held to the outer edges of the site. The courtyard, aside from the sound of children playing, is otherwise as quiet as a library.

▲ Figure 2.1.3

Operation Friendship, Edmonton,
Alberta 1984

D A six-unit triplex in a mature neighbourhood provides sunny walkout patios for lower level rental suites. Initially designed with the owner wanting to live in one of the units, the project costs increased by significant development levies, connection fees and site improvements imposed beyond the property line that change the proforma significantly. The owner now occupies a lower suite and uses it as an office while all of the other suites are rented.

E 'Plex' housing in Montreal, a sustainable and unique housing typology is important to the research. I speak to this housing model in Narrative 1.3 as it is a popular phenomenon in Montreal that impacts the BAAKFIL model relative to intergenerational living. The References also refer to a PhD dissertation (Parvarash, 2016) that examines this model in detail.

F Rudolf Schindler's House on Kings Road in Los Angeles is a major early departure from traditional residential architecture. A cooperative live/work space designed for two families (now widely referred to as co-housing), the building is pavilion-like with studio, living and utility spaces separated by sliding panels. With its tilt-up concrete walls, rooftop 'sleeping baskets' and extensive gardens, this residence is often cited as the first Modernist home in America.

G INFILLHAUS, an award winning infill prototype, increases density yet remains respectfully in scale with the street and its neighbourhood context. Lessons learned from Operation Friendship

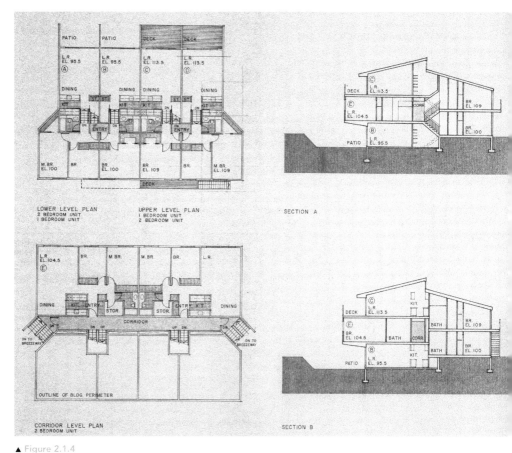

PATIO | PATIO | DECK | DECK

L.R. EL. 95.5 (A) | L.R. EL. 95.5 (B) | L.R. EL. 113.5 (C) | L.R. EL. 113.5 (D)

DINING | DINING | DINING | DINING

ENTRY | ENTRY

M.BR. EL. 100 | BR. | BR. EL. 100 | BR. EL. 109 | BR. | M.BR. EL. 109

DECK

LOWER LEVEL PLAN
2 BEDROOM UNIT
1 BEDROOM UNIT

UPPER LEVEL PLAN
1 BEDROOM UNIT
2 BEDROOM UNIT

SECTION A

DECK | L.R. EL. 113.5 (C)
(E) L.R. EL. 104.5 | CORR | BR. EL. 109
PATIO | L.R. EL. 95.5 | BR. EL. 100

L.R. EL. 104.5 (E) | BR. | M.BR. | M.BR. | BR. | L.R.

DINING | ENTRY | STOR. | STOR. | ENTRY | DINING

CORRIDOR

DN TO BREEZEWAY | DN | UP | UP | DN | DN TO BREEZEWAY

OUTLINE OF BLDG. PERIMETER

CORRIDOR LEVEL PLAN
2 BEDROOM UNIT

SECTION B

DECK | L.R. EL. 113.5 (C) | KIT.
(E) BR. EL. 104.5 | BATH | CORR | BATH | BR. EL. 109
PATIO | L.R. EL. 95.5 (B) | KIT. | BATH | BR. EL. 100

▲ Figure 2.1.4

Lakewood Apartments, Edmonton, Alberta 1981

(Project B) become another example in this project of respect for context that evolves as a response to the negative impacts of infill. The project is commissioned, but is also the subject of another design competition that precedes the Missing Middle Competition (Project A). As one of the smaller project examples in the competition it stands out for its respectful scale and spatial quality that yield design award recognition nationally but ignore the competition criteria based upon maximizing allowable density on the site. The project sends a message, but is not recognized in the competition.

H The Blatchford Masterplan, an international competition winner with Perkins & Will and Group2 Architecture, is central to the research. A future carbon neutral community for 25,000 people, it is a completely new 15 minute city from the 'mud up' with myriad sustainable systems and design features including a regional park, stormwater lake, historic preservation and a wide variety of housing types. Three years in the making, the masterplan uses urban design

◄ Figure 2.1.5
Triplex, Edmonton, Alberta 2018

guidelines and performance-based codes eschewing outdated zoning regulations. Municipal development strategies address land cost and density. Important to the research is an evaluation of the project's successes and failures. Blatchford is referred to as an example where a municipality acts as the developer. There are many lessons that foster debate about city making embedded in this project. The cost of land and its sustainable infrastructure is factored into the tender packages to developers for land parcels

'Plex' housing, Montreal, PQ

aiming to recover infrastructure costs as soon as possible rather than through other financing models such as municipal bond investment instruments, development agreements or arms-length development corporations. The land planning consultant on the project team at the time advocates that land be incorporated at its net present non-taxed value of zero dollars (the site is former city-owned municipal airport land) and to recoup its future value through the tax base and sales. This argument to stimulate the market is not accepted, despite support from the development community. This places the project behind its initial schedule of providing net zero living accommodation for 7500 people on site by 2019, with fewer than 100 units completed in 2022.

I The Kingsway Shopping Mall Masterplan, using the same team of consultants as Blatchford, and a similar 25-year gestation period, takes the learnings into the private sector to provide a different but applicable foundation for research into land economics and density. As an older but centrally located mall in The City of Edmonton, it is one of the most successful in the owner's portfolio. There is no pressure to develop the site immediately, thus the program is designed for the long-term view. The purpose of the Masterplan is to synchronize the owner's position—given the location of the site adjacent to Blatchford—to enable compatible and competitive mixed use growth as the market is stimulated by Blatchford. The owner is less encumbered by municipal governance regulations and is poised to offer land to outside developers at discount rates or to develop

◀ Figure 2.1.7

Schindler House, Los Angeles,
California

its residual land on its own, when the market warrants. It enjoys the ability to leverage its debt-free land holdings as it chooses and is well positioned to engage in new development with its Masterplan at any time. Land leveraging is key to the BAAKFIL business model and is deeply influenced by Projects H and I.

J As outlined in Narrative 1.3, personal experience—in hindsight—helps me understand myriad housing typologies at the outset of the research. This includes my own childhood home that in Canada today would be called a rental infill property. These memories clearly mark my subconscious decision making about neighbourhood, community and home.

K Similarly, our young family's former townhouse in False Creek, Vancouver, BC is an examination of other business models such as the co-op system. This project survives today as an example

INFILLHAUS, Edmonton,
Alberta 2016–17

Blatchford, Edmonton, Alberta
2011–13 (courtesy BJAL and P+W
Joint Venture)

of affordable, if not brilliant place-making. My family's ability to purchase a centrally located property in the heart of a redevelopment zone with transit and glorious views to the mountains with access to a public shoreline, i.e. everything Vancouver has to offer, could not be contemplated in the mid 1970s. This project, with a 60-year land lease (that is being renewed in ten years) is both a viable housing

Kingsway, Edmonton, Alberta
2014 (courtesy BJAL and P+W
Joint Venture)

model for all ages and an extraordinary example of affordable living
in the city. This is the missing middle, medium density housing—a
timeless manifestation of what the profession of architecture brings
to urbanization. While it is part of my reflection about BAAKFIL, the
co-op model is also explored as a result of Key Informant interviews
in Narrative 4.2.

The foregoing projects are critically important to the research.
In addition, a large body of work in my practice is community focused,
including public buildings, schools, other large housing projects
and urban design not mentioned. These are each influenced by a
commitment to public engagement, collaboration and respect. In
this context, it is a dilemma where we are rarely able to explore the
holistic idea of 'house and home' in smaller commissioned residential
projects, given the pressures of schedules, program and budgets.

Travel is also fundamental to the practice and its research
premise. Many projects involve field trips to cities and places around
the world including Western Europe, Britain, North America, China
and Australia. Field trips that influence the housing question are
conducted in connection with some of the listed projects and include

► Figure 2.1.11

Valois Infill, Montreal, PQ

► Figure 2.1.12

False Creek, Vancouver, BC

sustainable housing communities in Copenhagen, Denmark and Malmö, Sweden. An extensive exploration of zoning, missing middle housing and infill is undertaken in early 2022 from Edmonton, Calgary and Vancouver to Seattle, Portland, San Francisco and Los Angeles.

Collaboration within my community of practice also contributes to the learnings. Years of experience that coalesce though this work and combine with a commitment to community service, impacts my attitude toward people and place.

These influences—both positive and negative—together position me to undertake the challenge of what I am calling the housing question and marks my deep commitment to develop BAAKFIL.

2.2 Context

The housing question in Canada is a complex socio-cultural and economic problem of attainability, affordability and supply. Densification to reduce sprawl in respect of the environment and infrastructure cost and to increase supply is deemed central to addressing the myriad issues of housing people of all ages and income.

The marketplace responds with typologies that have been used for years—from single family dwellings to walk-up and high rise apartments. Innovation is elusive. Other mid-level approaches of varying density and scale, known as the missing middle, are historically restricted by antiquated zoning and municipal regulations. The cost of land today further impacts the ability of governments and developers to fully address the crisis in Canada.

The following excerpt from a CMHC design competition in 1979 (CMHC, 1979) illustrates that not much has happened since then.

In more recent years, it has become apparent that economic factors necessitate different kinds of shelter, particularly in the form of medium density housing. The National Housing Design Competition was held by its sponsors to seek excellent concepts for housing in Canada. More particularly, the sponsors wished competitors to address issues perceived to be of great new importance to Canada.

▼ Figure 2.2.1

Original Missing Middle diagram
(courtesy Opticos Design)

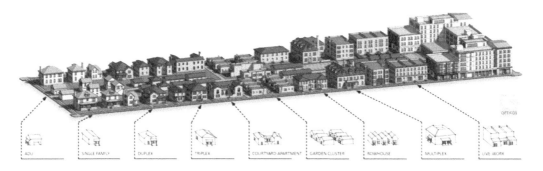

The first of these was increased density in residential neighborhoods.

Where former competitions held by CMHC had emphasized the importance of the well-designed single family house, this competition concentrated instead on more compact densities (of housing forms appropriate to sites in various regions) ranging from 25–75 dwelling units per hectare.

(Foreword and Professional Advisor's Introduction (edited), National Housing Design Competition 1979 (CMHC, 1979, pp. 5, 6))

The CMHC competition is a housing design challenge to architects from almost *45 years ago*. It is a clear reminder that densification of residential neighbourhoods in Canadian cities has failed to gain meaningful traction against the single family house building industry.

Housing cost increases are at crisis levels. The Canadian Real Estate Association announced on 15 April 2021 that the average cost for a single family home on its MLS system was $716,828 when including the inflated and landlocked markets of Toronto and Vancouver, a whopping increase of 31.6% over 12 months, the biggest annual pace of gain on record in Canada (Evans, 2021).

This problem is not restricted to larger centres. In its 17 May 2021 edition, the national publication *MacLean's* magazine reported that small town Canada meets the $1m threshold for single family housing with purchases several hundred thousand dollars over ask.

Newspapers, journals, magazines and the mainstream media cover the topic of the housing crisis regularly with examples and forecasts that illustrate the problem that impacts people of all backgrounds who appropriate the majority of their earnings to service housing debt. The problem is everywhere but is much more acute in some of Canada's more populous regions.

The graph in Figure 2.2.2 from RBC Economics illustrates just how far we have fallen into the affordability abyss in all our cities, but most notably Vancouver and Toronto.

Post pandemic, with inflation, higher interest rates and increased geopolitical unrest worldwide, the housing crisis in Canada continues to even higher stress levels than experienced at the outset of the research.

In May 2023, after house prices dropped during much of 2022, the Canadian Real Estate Association released its latest statistics that the average selling price of a home on its MLS system in April 2023 was $716,000 (Evans, 2023). This is now back to pre-pandemic levels and is an increase of more than $100,000 since January 2023.

These articles speak to the lack of supply and miss the point that the market offers little choice. Smaller product available for smaller households at lower price points is rare. This is an ongoing

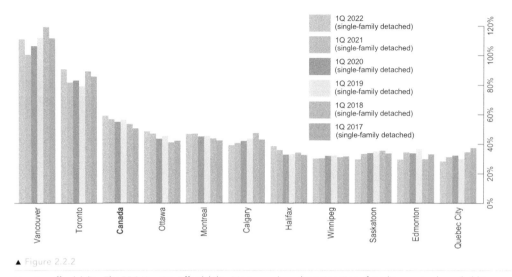

Legend:
- 1Q 2022 (single-family detached)
- 1Q 2021 (single-family detached)
- 1Q 2020 (single-family detached)
- 1Q 2019 (single-family detached)
- 1Q 2018 (single-family detached)
- 1Q 2017 (single-family detached)

Cities: Vancouver, Toronto, **Canada**, Ottawa, Montreal, Calgary, Halifax, Winnipeg, Saskatoon, Edmonton, Quebec City

▲ Figure 2.2.2

Housing affordability. The RBC Housing Affordability Measures show the proportion of median pre-tax household income that would be required to cover mortgage payments (principal and interest), property taxes and utilities based on the benchmark market price for single family detached homes and condo apartments, as well as for an overall aggregate of all housing types in a given market (Source: RBC Economics, Housing Trends and Affordability reports, accessed 21 July 2022)

scenario where industry and government continue to look through a very narrow tunnel, lamenting the lack of the status quo, single family house—from small town Canada to our larger centres.

Since the beginning of this exploration in late 2019, three major events—Covid-19, inflation and interest rate hikes have resulted in a more acute crisis in housing availability and affordability in Canada and across much of North America. In Canada, societal expectations for adequate shelter that were not being met earlier, are now seeing higher income earners such as teachers, nurses and other professionals unable to afford to purchase a house.

Since supply remains a major issue, governments at every level naturally claim the solution is to increase the housing supply at all costs, despite history demonstrating that dramatic increases in supply and demand generally result in increased prices.

Emerging Trends in Real Estate 2023, by PwC and ULI, provides an informed analysis of investment and development trends in context with the finance, capital markets and property sector marketplace in the United States and Canada. Its 2023 report, released in September 2022 (PwC, 2022) covers topics from Covid-19 and its impacts to geopolitical unrest, interest rates and the like. It concludes the housing supply issue must be dealt with 'from all angles' and that Canada 'does not have the capacity to meet housing demand'. We are in the middle of a major unresolved national crisis.

The Land Calculus

What is forgotten or ignored in this crisis is land cost.

Cities sell surplus land in the open market at the same retail market price as the development community to maximize return. While cities institute affordable housing strategies, they also contribute to the increase in land value. Figure 2.2.3 is a simple example—a vacant infill lot that requires city infrastructure upgrades at the owner's cost. The selling price equals the average cost of a single family dwelling in Edmonton at the time of offer in 2020. The site is beside a public stair and right of way but there are no sidewalks, the city street and hillside retaining wall is beyond its useful life, needing new drainage, and the back alley is not paved.

FOR SALE – RESIDENTIAL INFILL SITE

50′ Riverdale Infill lot

Edmonton

SUBJECT PROPERTY

$439,900

$439,900   10173 – 93 Street NW

Neighbourhood: Riverdale
Sale Land Legal Description: Lot 67, Block 1, Plan 2057Q
Holdings: 43822
File: CS180002
Total Land Area: 7,463 square feet (more or less)

Existing Land Use Zone: RF2 – Low Density Infill Zone

Last Update: December 2, 2020
Tax Roll Number(s): 3830353

Sector: Central

Buyers Application Form:
ONLINE FORM – FILL OUT & SEND [LINK]
PDF FORM [LINK] – DOWNLOAD, SCAN & E-MAIL

Estimate of 2020 Taxes: $4,290
(subject to verification by Assessment & Taxation)

PROPERTY INFORMATION:

• Incredible 50′ wide infill lot now available! This vacant 50′ by 150′ lot is located at the end of a cul-de-sac in the mature Riverdale Neighbourhood. The generous sized lot has great potential, and is suitable for a number of development options. The location offers great access to excellent amenities, including schools, river valley trails, Dawson Park and Downtown. All developments must conform with the Mature Neighbourhood Overlay and the Riverdale ARP.

• Interested parties are encouraged to review the Residential Infill Website about the many process changes and educational tools in progress to improve infill activities in mature neighbourhoods.

• All costs associated with the development of these lands including but not limited to roadway modifications, upgrading, modification/relocation of existing services, required by any new development will be borne by the Buyer.

▲ Figure 2.2.3

Municipal land offering

One of my Key Informants, KI*_8, cites his experience building hundreds of apartment and condominium units in Alberta where, he states, the cost of construction has not increased dramatically in a generation other than by keeping pace with the general cost of living. The cost of urban land during this same 25 year period has risen exponentially, making land cost a major barrier to housing affordability.

The densification agenda as it relates to infill in mature neighbourhoods is to increase the affordable housing supply and reduce (suburban) sprawl by allowing density increases on lots zoned for single family dwellings. This yields two unintended outcomes: protectionism of single family neighbourhoods against development altogether (e.g. Toronto's Yellowbelt (Lorinc, 2019)) and speculation whereby single houses are demolished with lots sold *at much higher land prices*, with two 'skinny' houses of equal or larger area to replace them, driving market prices even higher.

Both extremes *contribute* to the housing affordability crisis in Canada by increasing the value of land through exclusionary zoning and market speculation.

The numbers on the MLS listings, from my Key Informants and my own anecdotal evidence are consistent. Infill residences are more than $1m in 2023 in some areas in Edmonton (Infill, 2023); and in smaller cities. In larger centres like Toronto, one-off laneway infill projects since 2022 have exceeded $1.2m according to my KI_2. The average cost of a single family house in Kelowna, BC according to a colleague who moved there in early 2023 is $1.1m.

Land cost is always buried in these selling prices but it is a major factor. KI*_8 confirms that land in the mature neighbourhoods of Edmonton can account for up to 50% of the cost of infill today. This makes the land component the single biggest barrier to attainability and affordability. While the cost of purchasing a house in Canada has risen to crisis proportions, little has been written to differentiate the cost of building versus the cost of land.

This is discussed further in Narrative 4.2. This book does not intend to unpack a statistical analysis of the land cost issue. It is fundamentally relevant but the technical and market dynamic reasons why land cost is such a major barrier and what the actual amounts are from city to city is not the issue.

The issue for me is that it is simply a major barrier.

Given its relevance to the research question, however, I do conduct some general investigation on the impacts of this and the inability or unwillingness on the part of governments and large development companies to acknowledge the issue.

In response to the housing crisis, the Central Mortgage and Housing Corporation (CMHC), Canada's national housing agency is overseeing a major $300m Housing Supply Challenge Innovations Grant Program (CMHC, 2023), a five-year initiative inaugurated in 2020. CMHC does not even acknowledge land cost in a program specifically seeking innovations to overcome the barriers of housing supply. My application to CMHC for a program grant to investigate this matter specifically is not accepted.

As to the developer, it is common for these costs of course to be passed on to the consumer.

Two recent publications: *Sick City: Disease, Race Inequality and Urban Land* (Condon, 2021) and *Icebergs, Zombies and the Ultra Thin: Architecture and Capitalism in the Twenty-First Century* (Soules, 2021) come closer to discussing land cost but focus on socio-cultural phenomena rather than the impact of land cost on housing or real estate development. Condon makes connections especially during Covid-19 between disease, race and economic disparity (i.e. urban housing conditions). Soules obliquely connects land and architecture to what he terms 'finance capitalism', using specific architecture typologies such as the pencil thin condominium towers in New York City as investment vehicles.

The myth of land prices is explored in a paper published by UMASS Wealth Real Estate in August 2022 (Grantham, 2022). The author challenges the premise that there is not enough land on which to build in our cities and therefore high land cost is basically supported and accepted by real estate developers, politicians, even academics. He argues that while land may be scarce in places, this does not apply to every city and while prices vary from city to city, they generally follow the same pattern, the main differences being the economic base and relative affordability of a given location.

I understand how the price of land varies greatly across the country. Market value depends on many factors—the social and economic population metrics, employment and economic activity of the region, etc. Closer to one's home, proximity to schools and green space and other amenities impacts real estate prices as well. Supply of urban land is also problematic. Canada's housing prices have also been pushed up by *lack* of development where demand is strong. However, BMO questions whether supply is the culprit behind rapid house price inflation. History shows that building more and quickly does not mean costs will come down (Better Dwelling, 2022).

As an urbanist, I observe that geography of a given region impacts land cost as well. Cities that experience unfettered growth in all directions with no physical boundaries, e.g. the prairie city, generally own lower land values as it is generally more attainable. Other land-locked cities limit the extent to which the population can expand outwards, such as Vancouver, Toronto and Halifax, especially since WWII with the advent of the traditional suburb. These cities yield higher land values, given the constraints of mountains and water around their edges. This is a relevant phenomenon even at the fringe of the city since land value is relative. The less land available and the higher the density, the higher the relative value. This occurs on the fringe and in the centre.

Scarcity, availability and attainability are all contributors to housing cost. Our cities are woefully underutilized even in their central core. Vacant land held for speculation and, for example, used as parking lots in downtown cores are not uncommon. Residential neighbourhoods that see backyards used for storage or lying fallow are obvious missed opportunities. Land is available, but it is neither used efficiently nor incentivized for other purposes.

To bring these generalizations closer to my research objectives, Figure 2.2.4 and Figure 2.2.5 are map sketches that demonstrate typical inefficiencies. The illustrations show the block of my Demonstration Project No. 1 in the mature neighbourhood of Dovercourt, Edmonton. This is a typical single family block consisting of 50 foot wide standard lots and larger corner and pie lots, service alleys and city easement land to the west (left side). Excluding the surplus easement land, the area of single family zoning setbacks of front, side and rear yards is slightly greater than 40% of the total titled lot area (41 lots) of the block. When the area of residual backyard space inside the setback requirements is added to the total, the total area of underutilized land is a significant 71% of the titled lot area. (Lots with garages include garage area in the total.) The block density is 4.88 units/net acre (6.8 units/ha).

Government and large developers claim that increasing supply is a major factor in solving the housing crisis but the irony is that, in some sectors, supply (e.g. infill) actually contributes to the issue.

Speculative infill lots, which I cover next, are typically more expensive to purchase than the original single family lot if the house on it is demolished and the property subdivided. This is because one can build twice the area on a split property and sell 'on spec'. Demand is high. The builder constructs to the maximum allowed under the bylaws and sells at the highest possible price.

Supply is an issue but supply is directly impacted by land cost. Developers need to procure land in order to increase the supply of housing. This means everything from interim financing, re-zoning, subdivision and land development agreements etc., must be completed and approved before it is possible to build and feed the housing supply chain. Developer pressure on municipalities to remove barriers and expedite approvals is understandable in this context.

My objective frames a broad *desire path* for investigation but the dissertation focuses on a specific major barrier: the cost of land.

The outcome of this research posits that land cost is the major problem to be sorted before the supply question can be addressed.

What if the land is already there?
What if it is underutilized?
Is this a possible solution?

Two other peripheral but important considerations in identifying the problem space involve:

Densification and Neighbourhood Impacts
and
Zoning and the Idea of Respect

Densification and Neighbourhood Impacts

Housing densification and its role in city making is a relatively new phenomenon in Canada, targeted at underutilized single family mature urban neighbourhoods.

Older post-war neighbourhoods are now leafy, walkable, fine grained and quite urban. They are 'closer' to the centre of cities now, given the extent of outward sprawl, and are in demand. Neighbourhoods built through to 1970 are also ripe for missing middle options that increase density and are adaptable to changing demographics. We can bring new life into these neighbourhoods, particularly those now served by transit systems that promote less reliance on the automobile.

Densification in these areas usually begins with some form of infill. Ironically when the goal is to increase the housing supply, this more often than not begins with *demolition* of serviceable housing stock, increasing land cost for the redeployment of suburban standards often resulting in oversized, speculative development; negating original densification objectives to 'fill in' the open space gaps of neighbourhoods. Such disruption creates fear and antipathy when seen as disrespectful and financially out of reach of many who wish to move to these generally more compact, walkable urban settings. These unintended outcomes illustrate in Edmonton especially, but across the country, that infill is not about building community. (This research conclusion is not intended to disparage infill as a *concept*, but to merely point out its context and impact in established mature neighbourhoods.)

Infill is predicated upon the simple idea of doubling the density of a single family lot by subdividing it in favour of adding two single family dwellings in its place (i.e. skinny houses on skinny lots). Alternatively one can add a garden suite or laneway house to the rear of a property that is not subdivided, to achieve the same basic densification goal.

It is unfortunate that missing middle typologies championed by Daniel Parolek (2020) in his seminal book *Missing Middle Housing*, e.g. duplex, triplex, fourplex and mixed use service commercial buildings with housing above—common to neighbourhoods across North America prior to the end of WWII—are effectively eliminated from consideration with infill bylaws, despite their prior success. Zoning bylaws conceived 70 years ago with the post-war building boom and the advent of suburbia have changed little since the beginnings of that dream—single detached housing, yard, car, family.

Oversized, expensive speculative development often follows, since as previously stated, developers build to the maximum allowable under infill regulations. These projects built for the open market are seldom completed for a specific client but are built 'on-spec' and sold at the highest cost the market will bear. Neighbours observe change to their blocks and their neighbourhood with little or no consultation.

▲ Figure 2.2.4

Land Map—40% underutilized

▲ Figure 2.2.5

Land Map—71% underutilized

Infill with 10 foot ceilings and no yard space? This is just rude.

S. Mahler GGA Architects, Calgary AB

The topic of housing in mature neighbourhoods is framed by this context of disrespectful interventions and neighbourhood disruption, fuelled by the notion that *densification* of single family neighbourhoods is good for the city one way or another.

◄ Figure 2.2.6

Infill in Calgary (top) and Edmonton, Alberta (bottom)

Zoning and the Idea of Respect

Municipalities and consumers are used to the retail orientation of the housing industry. It is natural to assume that increasing supply in mature neighbourhoods calls upon the housing industry, which is a major driver of the Canadian economy, to solve the problem. As a commodified, product-driven industry, however, as illustrated in Figure 2.2.7, it is designed for large developments, not piecemeal interventions in mature neighbourhoods.

The housing industry is structured for large-scale development and offers little choice for, say, a single professional, a single parent or a multigenerational family. You can buy more than you need or adapt to rooms not designed for specific use.

But if new suburbs can address the increasing cost of development by building bigger product on smaller land parcels

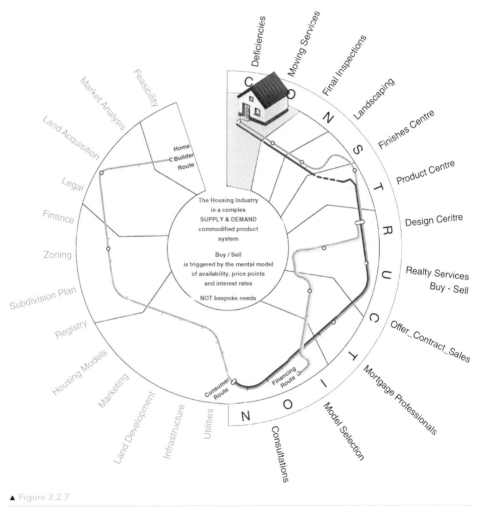

▲ Figure 2.2.7

Housing Industry

and incorporate townhouses and apartments alongside single family houses to increase density, why not in mature neighbourhoods? Here of course it is not new. That is the difference. Thus the industry ignores context and long-established socio-cultural patterns.

Second, traditional zoning regulations cannot recognize (or support) innovative densification options that are scalable. They separate uses and make it difficult to mix forms and different but compatible occupancies including multiple missing middle typologies—some that yield the fine grained, walkable communities that developed organically in the city pre WWII.

Finally, as a regulatory framework, zoning ignores the reality of changing *demographics*.

This is a serious problem, for example, with an older population. People wishing to move into a central mature walkable neighbourhood without a car to be closer to or to be with family have little choice but to consider illegal suites because of rigid regulations that negate multi-family options. This is an historically major problem with changing demographics, land cost and innovation.

Things are changing, however. In the face of the housing question, many cities in recent years embrace the idea of updated flexible zoning or zoning reform to move forward with the densification agenda.

In 2022, The State of Oregon legislated the removal of single family zoning altogether (Wamsley, 2019), encouraging densification. This includes the missing middle duplex or triplex units, depending upon eligibility criteria for such things as minimum lot size. The state, with Portland leading the way, is discouraging new single family housing. This recognizes changing demographics and therefore social, environmental and economic market influences. It does not mean this will improve the value of housing design, but it is a dramatic start.

Other cities like Minneapolis and Vancouver are following with programs and zoning reform of all descriptions. The City of Edmonton has allowed one-off garden suites and secondary suites for several years and eliminated residential parking minimum requirements. It aggressively approves a new Zoning Bylaw for January 2024, to allow more housing typologies—including eight dwellings or more apartment units on single family lots—without any community consultation.

Given the housing crisis, this zoning reform is actually changing its focus to encourage increased density, based on expediency and pressure to increase supply. This means removing barriers to the *developer*. I call this a new developer entitlement model.

The densification agenda requires respect to context, neighbourhood character and demographics—encouraging multi-generational living and aging in community. The housing emergency response changes that agenda to a much narrowed scope of putting product to market as soon as possible.

Neighbourhoods now risk further atomization with larger-scale development without consultation and demolition of mature housing, changing the scale and character of mature leafy streetscapes. Removing outdated zoning restrictions in favour of entitlements does not address the issue of zoning with respect for community.

This is going to be hard and there's no way of solving the affordable housing crisis that does not involve upsetting the neighbors.
21 October 2022—Mark Richardson, Housing Now, quoted in *The Globe* and *Mail*: Toronto's housing crisis is top of mind as the city heads to the polls.

Summary

This publication is all about the big idea of land cost; and its impacts.

These issues and a deeper interest in the housing question in my practice peak at the macro and micro levels of city making. Our precedent project masterplan (a joint venture) for the unoccupied Blatchford Municipal Airport Lands in Edmonton, Alberta, a regenerative community (beyond net zero) for 25,000 people over a planned build out of 25 years, is cited again here. Layering the three pillars of social, economic and environmental sustainability into a mixed use community, a 15 minute city is envisioned on vacant, undeveloped land. Next, but at the micro scale of neighbourhood infill, the previously mentioned INFILLHAUS is designed for a site in a mature, Edmonton inner city neighbourhood. Here the notion of respect to context is critically examined.

The impact of the cost of land as a barrier to attainability and affordability is manifested in these two projects. The Blatchford lands generate zero revenue for the city but land parcels are offered to developers at high market rates, justified by anticipating enormous future returns for the industry and of course, future value in municipal tax revenue. Twelve years later, fewer than 100 units of modest, stick frame town homes are complete, well below the forecast density of 7500 people by 2019 (Amato, 2022). The land cost could not be absorbed by the market and, unfortunately, no major developers participated. This despite the unrivalled enormous opportunity of an unencumbered site with proximity to an expanded LRT and five-minute journey to downtown; with shopping, health care and education facilities next door.

Even a modest construction budget could not offset the land cost in the INFILLHAUS neighbourhood. The total cost of the development at just under $800,000 in late 2017 was well beyond its market absorption limit and the project did not proceed.

Two examples at opposite ends of the development spectrum illustrate land cost as a major obstacle.

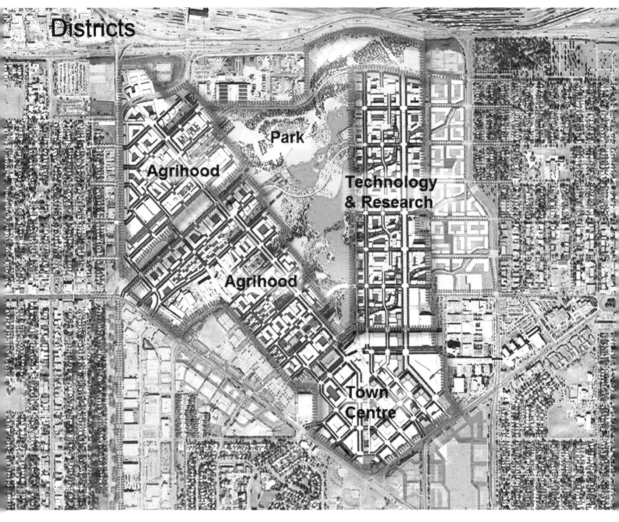

Districts

Park

Agrihood

Technology
& Research

Agrihood

Town
Centre

▲ Figure 2.2.8

Blatchford Masterplan Districts, Edmonton, Alberta (courtesy BJAL and P+W Joint Venture)

Blatchford Masterplan Features,
Edmonton, Alberta (courtesy
BJAL and P+W Joint Venture)

+ AGRIHOOD

Flyway Park

WEST ELEVATION AND MAIN ENTRY

EAST ELEVATION

INFILLHAUS

Edmonton, Alberta
Barry Johns (Architecture) Limited

In the sprawling city of Edmonton, sensitive infill dwellings are a rarity. Infillhaus, originally conceived as a competition prototype, explores the merits of compact, flexible living in the prairie capital. The single detached dwelling is half the width of its neighbours, contributing to urban densification in the leafy inner-city Norwood district.

The dwelling's bedrooms are embedded in the ground, using the natural insulating capability of the earth to maintain winter warmth and to provide cooling in the summer. The living space is contained above in a high-ceilinged, pavilion-like volume, zoned between "servant" and "served" spaces by tree-like structural columns. This floor overlooks the street and backyard, with no windows peering into adjoining lots. A thin, galvanized steel canopy extends over both ends of the building, providing a simple, contemporary lid and protection against the elements.

As a good neighbour, the house includes a raised entry and veranda to welcome visitors. It significantly reduces excavation and construction times by choosing a smaller footprint and opting against a full basement. The home aims to achieve net zero energy consumption—beginning with its building orientation that tracks and captures the sun's energy from east to west, and layering in an efficient envelope, building integrated photovoltaics, and a ground source heat pump.

Manon Asselin :: This is an incredibly refreshing and charming project. The proportions and connections are impeccable, and the design offers a surprising and unexpected solution to the need to integrate the house into the typology of the heritage neighbourhood. The architect has taken a mansion and sliced it down the middle, playing with a half profile to see what it could become.

Patricia Patkau :: The Infillhaus is carefully drawn and successful in its presentation. It is precisely calibrated to its tight lot, and you can see how light would get in everywhere. It reads as both a Japanese temple on the side façade and a strangely warped idea of a home on the front. It's done with such elegance, care and consideration, and is really a phenomenal little project.

David Sisam :: I am a real fan of the Charleston Single House typology, and this one-room-deep house reminds me of that model—particularly in its challenge to residual side yards and inappropriate scale. This house inverts the conventional arrangement of having bedrooms at the top, by placing them below and raising the living areas in a very eloquent way—a piano nobile taking advantage of the volume created by the roof form. The project has a very convincing and well-considered sustainability strategy. Most of all, the project is both highly rational (using served and servant spaces) and very elegant at the same time, as illustrated by the beautiful model and clear drawings.

▶ Figure 2.2.10

INFILLHAUS (courtesy *The Canadian Architect*)

SECTIONAL PERSPECTIVE

SOUTH ELEVATION

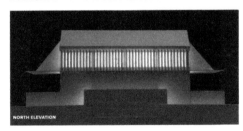

NORTH ELEVATION

BASEMENT

1 STORAGE
2 PATIO
3 BEDROOM / MEDIA / DEN
4 MECHANICAL
5 VERANDA / PORCH
6 LIVING SPACE
7 KITCHEN

MAIN FLOOR

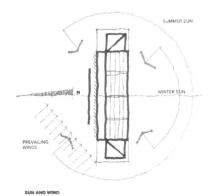

SUN AND WIND

OPPOSITE The detached infill house includes raised verandas at the front and rear. The main floor is a flexible open plan containing the home's living spaces, while bedrooms are on the lower level. **ABOVE, TOP TO BOTTOM** Tree-like structural columns create a gentle division between "servant" and "served" spaces on the main floor; photovoltaic panels are optimally tilted towards the south; the north elevation includes screens that filter light and protect against the prevailing winds.

2.3 Objective

My objective is to explore a practice-based solution through a new business model and an architectural design tool-kit to illustrate how this model can be applied. My interpretation of the housing question uncovers three specific areas of concern, beginning with the cost of land. My primary objective is to change the land calculus in the development of a new business model.

Two other objectives evolve from the same context analysis in Chapter 2.2. These are (1) to provide better development opportunities inside the densification agenda to address its impact on mature neighbourhoods and (2) to demonstrate how zoning renewal can maintain respect for existing mature neighbourhoods and the people who wish to age in their community. These are interconnected but I identify them separately as objectives against which the idea of the architectural design tool-kit can be evaluated.

The objectives identify the need for a business model to remove barriers to affordability, especially land cost.

The objectives identify the need for an architectural design tool-kit, promoting alternate housing typologies that address respect to context and changing demographics within the densification conversation.

Together these objectives need to address the housing question. What ultimately evolves from this journey is a new housing/land acquisition model called BAAKFIL.

An overarching objective is to advance new knowledge within the profession of architecture. The realization that architects are outliers in the housing industry is a serious concern. Despite much to say about low density sprawl, design quality and making cities, our audience remains comparatively small. Constrained by outdated zoning bylaws, planning regulations and risk averse financial structures, it is understandable that industry yields little incentive for professional design and innovation.

My goal with BAAKFIL is to change the narrative.

2.4 Methodology

Design science research (DSR) is a methodology used in the Doctor of Design and is the foundation for the evolution of BAAKFIL (Pello, 2018). The Key Informant participant role distinguishes this methodology. Subject matter experts are chosen and provide input to help establish and/or verify the research context at the beginning of the work. The process culminates in an objective peer review conducted by the same experts as the work is nearing completion, thus closing the circle of inquiry, providing an opportunity for reflection and then determining what to do next. I describe this in more detail on the following pages.

The evolution of BAAKFIL also includes using one's own work as a precedent alongside the work of others to influence the research. This too is an exercise in evaluation and reflection.

Working within the profession of architecture involves collaboration within a Community of Practice (CoP) comprised of clients, consultants, contractors, regulators and others who offer continuous and often expert opinion on real projects that are the subject of the research question. This is the day to day.

The overlap of these inputs informs the research and development of BAAKFIL and this is further discussed in Chapter 7 Conclusion.

I interpret the way in which the Key Informants participate with the research in Figure 2.4.1.

▶ Figure 2.4.1

Key Informant diagram

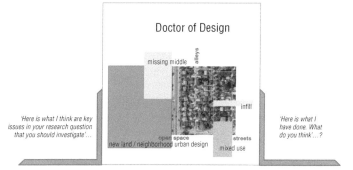

Subject matter experts provide an overarching 'umbrella' at the outset, to help focus the research.

A peer review as the work nears completion closes the circle of inquiry and contributes to the creation of new knowledge.

Key Informant 'bookend' role – helping to set the research context at the beginning and doing an objective peer review of the work at the end

My research objective and project enjoys a strategic connection with the key informant process. As I describe, the process evolves after the first round of interviews into a somewhat hybridized methodology where the combination of the formal key informant (KI) expertise and informal key informant (KI*) input through my CoP is cross pollinated in the development of BAAKFIL.

The selection of Key Informants occurs soon after the initial research is under way with the problem setting exercise. In order to achieve a clear objective and understanding of a manageable scope of work, the process involves the identification and selection of subject matter experts connected in some way to the main research objective. Individuals with different backgrounds and expertise assist my quest to understand the scope of work—in my case the complex world of the housing industry and the housing question. In practice, this opportunity is rare, given typical commissioned project boundaries of schedules, budgets and program.

While there is much published literature about housing in North America, there is surprisingly little attention paid to what eventually becomes central to the research: *the cost of land as a major barrier* to attainability and affordability. Readings I consider relevant are referenced throughout, but it seems I occupy a space where new knowledge is predicated upon discovery in this area; rather than the assimilation of information already available. In other words, while I review significant material about the housing question, the industry and its myriad influences, there is no equal measure of material about practical working models that propose what to do about it and how, especially with respect to land cost.

To close this gap and to broaden my knowledge of the subject, I choose a total of seven people to interview under the IRISS (IRISS, n.d.) ethics procedures. The questions at the outset encourage each Key Informant to speak to the issues holistically, with freedom to deepen the conversation relative to their own experience and expertise. This methodology helps me understand the complex problem space of housing as a topic and my primary goal—dealing with land cost and facilitating affordability. The KI process opens the door to new knowledge and points me to other experts to develop an original creative solution. Five other experts participate in the interview process but, for business or personal reasons, decline the formality of the IRISS documentation. I nevertheless subject these individuals to the same IRISS ethics principles including the semi-structured interview questions, although I meet with them on several occasions. In addition, instead of recording these sessions, I take copious notes and archive numerous emails, journals and correspondence and organize the content in a secure storage location. This occurs over several months.

Some are contacted on an as required basis to review the progress. The banker is a good example. Others stay in contact throughout the research period and (by declining the formal IRISS process) assume a role in my CoP. Others review the work only as it nears completion. Given their different backgrounds, the input is diverse but filled with overlap and common interests. While not originally contemplated, this hybridized outcome enriches the research.

The Key Informant experts are:

KI_1   architect and author
KI_2   architect
KI_3   urban designer and planner/landowner
KI_4   planner
KI_5   urban advocate
KI_6   non-profit developer
KI_7   community advocate

'Qualified' Key Informant experts KI* (i.e. non IRISS) are:

KI*_8   for-profit developer
KI*_9   executive of a major public bank

KI*_10   legal counsel
KI*_11   client/consumer
KI*_12   mentor/Professor Emeritus

KI_1 is a published author, architect and Professor of Architecture at a major Canadian University School of Architecture with a reputation for affordable housing strategies.

KI_2 is an architect, urbanist and expert in the field of innovative wood construction and an advocate for building equality in the profession of architecture. Her practice focuses on housing for aging populations.

KI_3 is an urban designer, planner and a public policy maker for urban development, zoning and densification in a major Canadian city. He also contributes to the research as a landowner.

KI_4 is a planner with particular expertise around infill housing and missing middle housing.

KI_5 is an urban advocate and civil society leader in cities across Canada and the USA. She is an expert on the work of Jane Jacobs.

KI_6 is a non-profit developer of micro unit rental and special needs housing. Trained as an architect, he is Executive Director of a community housing corporation and formerly a project manager with a major housing developer in Canada and project manager for a municipal Innovative Housing Lab.

KI_7 is a community advocate who oversees a network of urban community leagues, each committed to building healthy neighbourhoods.

The five additional interviewees I identify as 'qualified' Key Informants (KI*) for clarity.

KI*_8 is a for-profit developer and former client with 25 years of experience in multi-family and condominium housing projects. Consulting independently; he is involved in all aspects of the Alberta marketplace inside the housing industry.

KI*_9 is a senior executive of a large public bank in Canada overseeing a real estate portfolio of $5.5bn. Extended interviews include an associate executive who addresses the minutiae of the banking industry as it applies to the research.

KI*_10 is senior partner of a law firm and legal counsel for my practice, who alongside one of his associate partners, assists in vetting the legal implications of the research objectives and business model.

KI*_11 is a client introduced to my practice prior to the beginning of the doctoral research, engaging me to undertake an infill project as a result of previously published work in the practice. As husband and wife professionals, both embrace the idea of the research and contribute to it based on their direct experience in the infill marketplace and the pursuit of land.

KI*_12 is Professor Emeritus of a major Canadian university's school of architecture who during the preparation of the skeletal thesis framework agrees to participate in an informal peer review of the work, having been introduced to it only after the research is deemed complete and the creative project is well under way. This review focuses on the idea of future-proofing BAAKFIL, impacting the reflections in Chapter 7 Conclusion.

The formal IRISS semi-structured interviews take place during June and July 2021. Each interview is recorded, with video and transcripts held in secure storage. The informal KI*s are documented as previously described with data also held in secure storage. Interviews include the following general questions to initiate the proceedings, allowing the participants to address these and any other topics freely during the interview:

The following sample research questions are a guide to frame the interview. Semi-structured interviews are conversational to enable the interviewee freedom to elaborate informally.

What are the specific factors that influence your experience and impact your business/situation/ community?

1.1 How does cost (land, construction, financing), the regulatory framework (zoning, infrastructure services, surcharges, processes, time) and the market affect your experience?
1.2 What are your priorities and challenges?
1.3 What key issues should be further investigated?

What are your experiences with the densification agenda, neighbourhood development and acceptance?

1.4 What is your expectation for development in the neighbourhood or community?

1.5 What do you measure, aspire to or look for in a neighbourhood development?
1.6 How does the regulatory framework fit into this context?
1.7 What key issues should be further investigated?

Given that land and construction/infrastructure costs are major factors that impact affordability,

1.8 What other mitigating factors do you experience?
1.9 How do you approach affordability?
1.10 How do you address the notion of flexibility?
1.11 Describe your market experience regarding right sized, housing typologies in the context of changing demographics, e.g. aging population, smaller families and single occupant households?
1.12 What key issues should be further investigated?

What am I missing?

The process informs the wording of the research question and shapes the structure of the research.

The research question is: *How can my practice deliver sustainable densification innovations that address attainability, affordability, demographics, bespoke needs and societal expectations while being respectful to place?* (Note: The question is developed after analysing the housing industry, its impact on the growth of cities and residual impacts on densification agendas, particularly in older mature neighbourhoods. This work, while important to my understanding of the problem space and part of creating BAAKFIL, is eventually situated peripherally to the primary research objective—land cost.)

The initial KI interviews help me to focus on critical areas to meet the research objectives. The overarching goal that evolves is to measure the metrics of land and housing cost, the zoning/

densification agenda and establish a practice model that respects consumers, residents and community value sets in mature urban neighbourhoods.

I include several key informant observations and challenges in this chapter to illustrate the primary takeaways from these interviews. Sidebar quotations emphasize points of discussion where appropriate.

My interest in the morphology of the industry pivots to that of the difference between laws and rules; governance and community self-determination. KI_5 and KI_7 encourage me to investigate these parameters. Similar observations are reflected upon in Narrative 1.3 given that KI_5 also raises these matters during the first DDes cohort symposium. The re-affirmation of its importance becomes a major objective in the development of BAAKFIL as a self-regulated micro-community model, beginning with the preservation of existing housing and landowner agency.

KI_2 and KI_3, from differing perspectives arrive at the same conclusion regarding zoning as a limiting barrier to densification of mature neighbourhoods. The consequences of infill are driven in large part by new zoning that at the outset of the research only permits certain infill typologies, such as subdividing single family lots and permitting secondary suites and garden suites. Other more flexible options are restricted. This is complicated by the factor of risk and the reluctance of the banking industry to embrace one-off development, versus the larger-scale development projects common in subdivisions. This becomes a significant objective—to learn more about the banks. This leads me on a journey that validates the KI observations, as the two largest Canadian chartered banks show no interest in speaking with me about the research; while a major public bank, recognizing an entrepreneurial opportunity, embraces the subject. As a result, in Narrative 4.2, the input from KI*_9 and his associate VP is pivotal to the development of the BAAKFIL business plan.

The role of the municipality and the advent of densification bylaws written over the past 15 years is explored in detail with KI_4. The message in promoting densification is developer driven, concerned with setbacks, height, bylaw enforcement. In Edmonton, from the time this begins in 2008 up to 2018, this yields some interesting innovations. The City of Edmonton Infill Road Map 2018 includes a 25 foot minimum lot allowance, garden suites and elimination of parking minimums. Innovations also yield unintended consequences—such as increased market value of land and recognition that the bylaws focus on regulations, not design. As a result, two design competitions (previously referenced in Chapter 2.1) are held to bring design into the conversation—both for infill (2016) and for the missing middle (2019) that enable mixed use including small-scale neighbourhood commercial use.

In each case the competition is designed to maximize density and justify land value according to the infill bylaws and expectations of the City Real Estate Department.

Great world cities have a large vocabulary of housing options. Demographics give Canada justification for a vocabulary of options.

– KI_1

An internal post mortem summarizes both positive and negative consequences.

The role of the developer, and the subject of profitability within the existing regulatory framework is discussed throughout with KI_1, KI_6, KI_3, KI_4 and KI*_8.

KI_1 sees the development community as a contradiction between differing objectives—regulatory frameworks to encourage growth but with controlled oversight, to developer profit orientation, to affordability issues with consumers—the challenge to me is to navigate between these worlds.

KI_6 and KI*_8 analyse the sustainability of their developer business from a non-profit and a for-profit perspective.

Most importantly, the overarching theme that comes out of the first round of key informant interviews is the common admission about the lack of discussion about the high cost of land.

This subject covers the gamut from the burden of additional fees, permits, connection charges and municipal development levies in the densification agenda to the artificiality of land value.

KI_3 confirms that municipalities are not interested nor do they examine the total costs of a developer proposal. Improvement levies, connection fees, development charges and land are all addressed within a siloed departmental structure and a policy-driven administration.

The assumption about total cost is always that the private sector does this work. Within the municipal structure it does appear this is an issue for planners; however, according to KI_4, internal policy still militates against a holistic examination of these impacts. I am told that one of the best things I can provide with my work is a project proforma.

With little incentive to change, this also becomes a manifestation of the housing industry zeitgeist where development cost increases are simply absorbed and passed on as they occur to the next party in line—land developer to property developer to construction suppliers and contractors to, ultimately, the consumer.

I am reminded of the quotation attributed to Richard Blythe (Blythe, 2021) during a 2021 Symposium keynote lecture. He speaks to the idea of tacit knowledge becoming 'white hot'. This is what happens when a collective of experts speaking independently, enable me to synthesize random but overlapping ideas alongside my own tacit knowledge and experience into an exciting and coherent structure of investigation and discovery.

Initially, however, this journey begins like one into a nether-world of completely different and conflicting value sets. Only through this process, however, am I able to put together a roadmap of the development process to yield, as a result, innovations of ways and innovations of things to address the research objective and the housing question.

The second round of interviews is addressed after the presentation of the demonstration projects in Chapter 6.2.

We likely put the land value in (for the Missing Middle competition) too high to achieve what we were looking for.

– KI_4

Land cost is what the market will bear. It is not real, it is fabricated.

– KI_6

References

Amato, S. (2022, October 12). Blatchford review ordered after project fails to meet expectations. CTV News. https://edmonton.ctvnews.ca/blatchford-review-ordered-after-project-fails-to-meet-expectations-1.6106707

Better Dwelling. (2022, July 19). *The Canadian real estate bubble's supply shortage myth is unraveling: BMO.* www.betterdwelling.com/the-canadian-real-estate-bubbles-supply-shortage-myth-is-unraveling-bmo/

Blythe, R. (2021). *Virginia Tech PRS4.* Washington, DC: Virginia Tech.

City of Edmonton. (2020, December 7). www.edmonton.ca/city_government/city_vision_and_strategic_plan/city-plan.aspx

CMHC. (1979). *National Housing Design Competition.* ISBN 0–662–50505-0, Cat. No. NH17–8/1979.

CMHC. (2023, May 16). Housing Supply Challenge. cmhc-schl.gc.ca/en/professionals/project-funding-and-mortgage-financing/funding-programs/all-funding-programs/housing-supply-challenge

Condon, P. (Ed.) (2021). *Sick city: Disease, race inequality and urban land.* Vancouver, BC, Canada: James Taylor Chair UBC.

Evans, P. (2021, April 15). Average price of Canadian home rising at fastest annual pace ever, now up to $716,828. CBC News. www.cbc.ca/news/business/crea-housing-march-1.5988543

Evans, P. (2023, May 15). Average Canadian house price rose to $716,000 in April—up by $100K since January. CBC News. www.cbc.ca/news/business/crea-housing-data-1.6843592

Grantham, D. (2022, August). Comparing farmland and urban land prices in Canada. *UMASS Wealth*, West Vancouver Property.

Infill. (2023, May 16). infill-edmonton.com/listings/?listing_price=900001–1250000&listing_neighborhood=&listing_year=

IRISS. (n.d.). University of Calgary. https://research.ucalgary.ca/conduct-research/additional-resources/iriss-human-ethics-and-animal-care

Lorinc, J. (2019). The stability trap. In A. Bozikovic (Ed.), *House divided.* Toronto: Coach House Books.

Parolek, D., with Nelson, A. C. (2020). *Missing middle housing: Thinking big and building small to respond to today's housing crisis.* Washington, DC: Island Press.

Parvarash, P. (2016). Montreal's superposed flats_the influence of architecture on...sense of place...Verdun Borough. PhD Thesis, Université du Québec à Montréal, Montreal. www.archipel.uqam.ca/9446/1/D3199.pdf

Pello, R. (2018, October 31). Medium. https://medium.com/@pello/design-science-research-a-summary-bb538a40f669

PwC. (2022, September). Emerging trends in real estate. pwc.com/ca/en/industries/real-estate/emerging-trends-in-real-estate.html

Soules, M. (Ed.) (2021). *Icebergs, zombies and the ultra thin* (p. 239). New York City: Princeton Architectural Press.

Wamsley, L. (2019, July 1). Oregon legislature votes to essentially ban single-family zoning. NPR. www.npr.org/2019/07/01/737798440/oregon-legislature-votes-to-essentially-ban-single-family-zoning

BAAKFIL

3.1 Introducing BAAKFIL

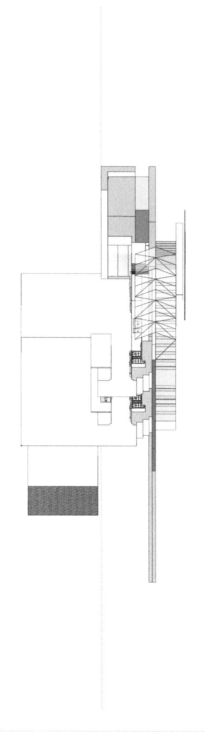

BAAKFIL Infrastructure Core

Learnings from the research and the first key informant interviews, confirm that the wicked problem that underpins the research is the cost of land. All other aspects of the research question reside inside a solution to this issue. To achieve this, the dissertation comprises three separate but essential initiatives.

A developer/owner **Business Model** and proforma addresses attainability and affordability of an alternative typology to infill densification in mature urban neighbourhoods.

An architectural **Design Tool-kit** demonstrates how the Business Model is deployed to promote densification and respect to context.

Two **Demonstration Projects** test the Business Model and Tool-kit as proof of concept.

To support the evolution of more affordable housing, the research addresses each of these initiatives separately, but interrogates them holistically to frame the body of work as an architectural design trilogy.

The *first step* in applying the research is to promote retention, not demolition of serviceable housing in mature urban neighbourhoods.

This achieves three simple, significant goals.

1. The first is to recognize the unintended negative consequences of traditional infill as a model for increasing the density of neighbourhoods. Demolition of housing is now a fundamental component of infill; ironically predicated on *removal* of housing first, then replacement with two or more units on the same property, thus doubling its density. This increases development cost as demolition and the discarding of re-useable building materials and products can be worth up to hundreds of thousands of new dollars. This cost is passed on to the consumer. Reuse is thus easy to justify in this context.
2. Retention, renovation or adaptive re-use is a more responsible approach to a densification, affordability and sustainability agenda. It is argued that responsible stewardship of the existing housing environment is important to combat climate change.
3. The removal of serviceable housing in mature neighbourhoods for new product changes its character. People who live in the same place for decades are either displaced or, experience changes to their personal social network that are out of their control. These impacts can contribute antipathy and fear towards neighbourhood change. Retention mitigates these issues.

Suffice to say that decades of dealing with community development in my practice proves that fear and antipathy emanates from uncertainty and a lack of trust that municipalities take such granular neighbourhood issues to heart.

The Statistics Canada Census released in 2022 (Statistics Canada, 2022) proves that Canada is an older population with increasingly

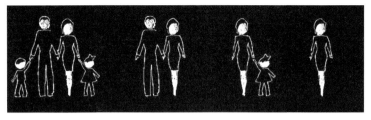

2022 Census, Household forecasts

smaller households. We are not an aging population any longer. More than 22% of Canadians are over 55 years of age and 19% are over 65. Moreover, the statistics also posit the majority of households in Canada in 25 years will be one person. The home building industry continues to build large product in new developments, including infill in mature neighbourhoods, by and large ignoring these staggering demographic forecasts.

The achievement of these goals enables solutions to other macro challenges—to remove barriers, negate displacement, increase affordability and choice, introduce a new business idea to the marketplace and promote granular level community organization and acceptance.

This is achieved by:

- retaining an original house and backfilling new housing on underused properties to yield smaller densification options that align with a changing demographic.
- developing a backyard strategy where underutilized land is fractionalized and made available for development, maintaining street and neighbourhood character and urbanistic intentions.
- creating a new business model about equity leveraging to unlock the potential of this underutilized land; where the landowner partners with a developer by contributing backyard space for development while retaining tenure in the original house and property. The developer builds new housing without the need to finance land. *Land cost is removed from the project proforma, substantially reducing development costs and instantly increasing affordability for the consumer.*
- equity leveraging to yield income for the landowner without putting up any cash and without having to move.
- benefitting the consumer with lower land cost since only land under a new unit is purchased.
- better utilization of city alleys as skinny yield streets with a sidewalk, addressing, promoting more activity, safety, social supports and small scale, community mixed use.
- promoting city building via neighbourhood revitalization, giving agency to residents to self-organize.

▲ Figure 3.1.3

BAAKFIL precedent projects—Lakewood Apartments, Triplex, INFILLHAUS (courtesy of *The Canadian Architect*) and Blatchford Masterplan, Edmonton, Alberta (courtesy BJAL and P+W Joint Venture)

Each of these principles is explored in the following chapters to describe a new, scalable housing paradigm called **BAAKFIL.**

Edmonton's new City Plan aspires to smart growth of up to 2 million people in the future—a density agenda of 42 units/ acre (105 units/ha). I anticipate the ability of the BAAKFIL model to re-frame how a neighbourhood can be gently reborn. If only 25% of single family lots in Edmonton's mature neighbourhoods commit to BAAKFIL over 25 years, a population increase in the hundreds of thousands is possible or, millions across the country. This is a non-aggressive, unthreatening and gentle approach to the densification agenda over time.

So where does BAAKFIL come from?

From the macro city scale of master planning, a regenerative— beyond net zero—community for 25,000 people over 25 years, to flexible multigenerational ground-oriented missing middle typologies in mature neighbourhoods, to infill; I reflect upon years of precedent work to stimulate a design process where the housing industry can be involved in the solution, rather than function as a barrier to innovation.

Working within the system, including the banking industry by leveraging existing land equity, I believe BAAKFIL can evolve to fit into an acceptable community development model. Here, industry and community can come together to drive a more ethical and, by example, pedagogical framework for development.

This is a densification model that (1) does not displace existing residents who wish to age in their community (2) enables landowners to monetize their largest asset—which is usually their personal property—and (3) contributes to the systemic growth of resilient, liveable cities.

Unlike one-off laneway or garden suites, BAAKFIL is a scalable typology, adaptable across the country with a defined business model. Land cost, lack of choice, attainability and affordability, maintaining and building community are each addressed with BAAKFIL, removing significant barriers to the housing supply challenge.

BAAKFIL is largely non-numeric and non-quantitative in that it does not concern itself with units per acre. It uses the term gentle densification *qualitatively*, to point to the need for a holistic approach that can still accommodate significant increases in the population with a focus on redeeming socio-cultural value.

As such, **BAAKFIL** is an acronym that describes:

Back Alley Advantage
Kinship
Family &
Integrated Living

References

Jacobs, J. (1961). *The Death and Life of Great American Cities.* New York: Vintage Books, Random House Publishing.

Statistics Canada. (2022). *Census of population.* www12.statcan.gc.ca/census-recensement/index-eng.cfm

BAAKFIL Business Model

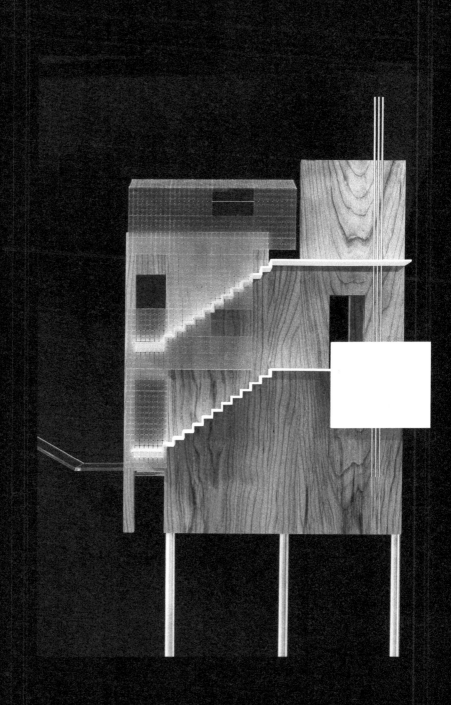

4.1 Business Model

The previous chapter discusses retention of existing housing in mature neighbourhoods.

This becomes the basis for an innovative approach to future development within the densification agenda.

This chapter describes the design of a new business model (*innovation of ways*)—that supports development of attainable and more affordable housing in response to the research findings. Combined with the findings that Canada 'does not have the capacity to meet housing demand', an idea known for some time in the housing industry and confirmed as previously referenced by PwC and ULI in 2022, I conclude that land cost is the critical, albeit ignored factor to mitigate the inflationary cost spiral of the housing question.

This investigation should also address the housing supply challenge.

I also conclude that a bold approach is needed to address this wicked problem:

Find a way to take land cost out of a development proforma.

If the cost of land is removed from a development equation altogether, this completely changes the metrics of densification. Major savings in *time* (assembling and subdividing land) and *money* (time costs, financing or purchasing costs) and the resulting reduction of *risk* (opportunity cost) can quickly improve the developer housing supply chain while savings can be passed on to the consumer—since the developer would not need to absorb this financial burden as an up-front cost.

It begins with a bare land condominium structure. Here consumer cost is also reduced, immediately, since it is not necessary to purchase 50% of a full titled lot subdivided for infill and sold at inflated prices. In a bare land condominium model, only the land under a new unit is purchased and the lot is held in common.

▼ Figure 4.1.1

Future streetscape possibilities

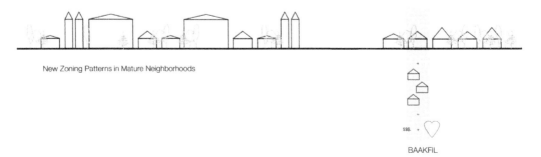

New Zoning Patterns in Mature Neighborhoods

BAAKFIL

This chapter explores the concept of landowner equity leveraging, and how land cost removal in a new business model can be achieved.

By leveraging equity in one's holdings—staying in place, keeping a house and retaining tenure in the property—the landowner can monetize the asset. Most people who own property, often the largest investment they ever make, never have an opportunity to redeem and use its value while remaining in situ and calling it home. By investing underutilized backyard land for development, the landowner becomes a partner with a developer in the company (the Devco) that builds the project.

By retaining ownership of the main house, staying in place to age in the community where many spend decades, instead of selling and buying elsewhere (at higher cost) and moving, the landowner is the first beneficiary who sees an immediate return on investment in the Devco partnership when the newly constructed units are sold, or rented. Income from the asset, without giving it up and without putting up any cash, is a compelling opportunity for any landowner. Even if the landowner has debt against the property, this debt can be refinanced and ultimately cleared through the investment proceeds.

The developer is a beneficiary when the cost of doing business is reduced in time and money, enabling more projects to be developed at the same time, with less risk. The consumer is a beneficiary when savings are reflected in the actual sales price. The market is a beneficiary with more sales at an affordable cost. The neighbourhood is a beneficiary with respectful densification.

Smaller product built in accordance with the demographic realities of smaller households importantly means neighbourhoods are not demolished for infill or larger-scale development.

In summary, the business model achieves the following:

- The cost of financing land to the developer is eliminated.
- With multiple projects at the same time, an existing or a new Devco can grow with minimal initial capital investment.
- Projects can still be traditionally financed.
- The cost of land to the consumer is mitigated by only purchasing the land under a new unit such as in a bare land condominium.

While a bare land condominium idea is not new, this is a new way of using a tried and tested model. It owns the scalable potential of city making since this can be deployed across the country. In a similar context, it is also possible to frame the business model for a rental/co-op scenario, also described in this chapter.

The City of Edmonton has 80+ mature urban neighbourhoods, i.e. communities largely built out by the mid 1970s when the construction of back alleys is superseded by outer-lying subdivisions with their cul de sacs and crescents. In each of these neighbourhoods, there are common lot sizes that range from 30 x 120 feet (9m x 36.5m) to 50 x 150 feet (15m x 45.7m). Every neighbourhood has corner lots and what is known as a 'pie lot', typically found on the outer side of continuous 'L' shaped streets as they turn a corner. Many cities across the country are founded on these same planning principles.

If a 25% absorption rate of new development occurs on pie, corner and 30–50 foot lots over a 25 year period (a generation), the population increase in Edmonton could exceed 250,000 people. If a 25% absorption occurs on pie lots alone, this amounts to 25,000 people.

I call this 'gentle' densification and it is referred to here as

25 in 25 in 25

This is significant when considering the relative gentle intervention and scale of the initiative, compared with the capital cost intensive precedent Blatchford Masterplan on 550 acres of unserviced land close to the city core that aspires to the same concentration of 25,000 population over 25 years.

Considered as a scalable idea in the context of the country, the potential yield is in the millions of population growth, a staggering

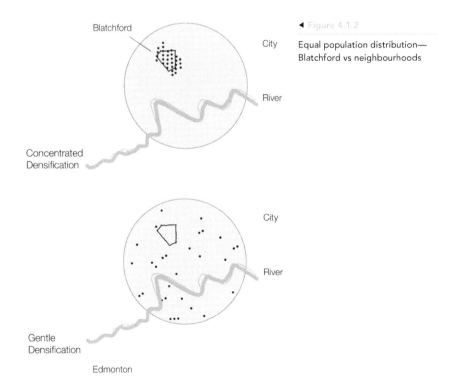

Blatchford

City

River

Concentrated
Densification

City

River

Gentle
Densification

Edmonton

◀ Figure 4.1.2

Equal population distribution—
Blatchford vs neighbourhoods

▲ Figure 4.1.3

Density Map: Gentle Densification

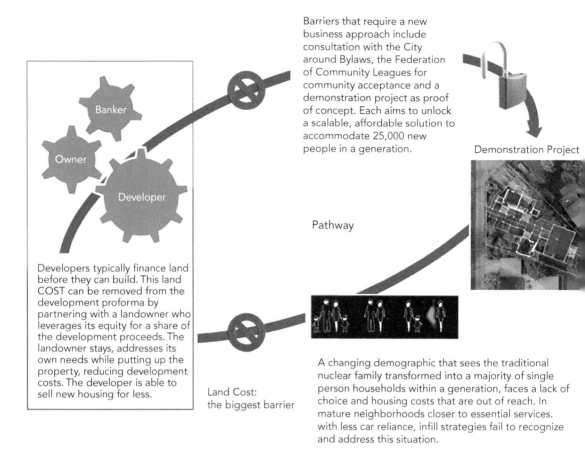

Barriers that require a new business approach include consultation with the City around Bylaws, the Federation of Community Leagues for community acceptance and a demonstration project as proof of concept. Each aims to unlock a scalable, affordable solution to accommodate 25,000 new people in a generation.

Demonstration Project

Pathway

Developers typically finance land before they can build. This land COST can be removed from the development proforma by partnering with a landowner who leverages its equity for a share of the development proceeds. The landowner stays, addresses its own needs while putting up the property, reducing development costs. The developer is able to sell new housing for less.

Land Cost: the biggest barrier

A changing demographic that sees the traditional nuclear family transformed into a majority of single person households within a generation, faces a lack of choice and housing costs that are out of reach. In mature neighborhoods closer to essential services. with less car reliance, infill strategies fail to recognize and address this situation.

▲ Figure 4.1.4

Business Model pathway

increase in a generation, on existing developed, serviced and— found—urban land.

This is gentle densification, attainable and more affordable; the conceptual framework of the business plan.

A series of illustrations (see Figures 4.1.3, 4.1.5 and 4.1.6) explain the idea of gentle densification on a typical neighbourhood block, followed by mapping the basic principles of the business model for condo and rental/co-op options, as an *innovation of ways*.

Figure 4.1.3 uses the same block in Dovercourt, also illustrated in Chapter 2.2, showing a total of 41 single family lots.

Yellow hatching illustrates 25% absorption of backyard space on this block over a 25-year period, using 11 standard, corner and

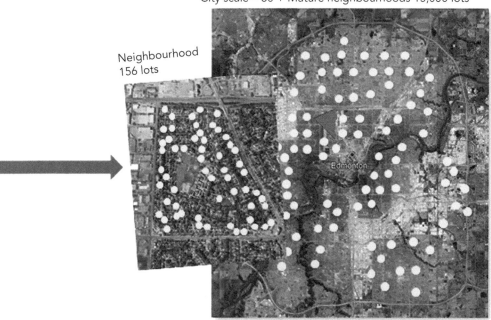

City scale – 80 + Mature neighbourhoods 15,000 lots

Neighbourhood
156 lots

Land cost is eliminated for developer and
mitigated for the consumer.

pie lots chosen at random. This represents gentle densification of up
to 24 standalone additional units for a total of 65 units on the block
based on two new units per standard lot and three new units per pie
lot. The new unit count increases to a maximum of 48 if each contains
the option of a lower rental suite or a small-scale neighbourhood
commercial space such as a hair salon.

This yields an average density range of 6.97–8.23 units/acre
(17.2–20.28 units/ha) for the block. This is roughly 20% of the City of
Edmonton densification agenda with 25% absorption over 25 years.

The red circle denotes the site of the pie lot Demonstration
Project No. 1 in Chapter 6.1.

Interestingly, if the same 11 lots are demolished for infill, there
is a zero net unit gain based on 22 new units minus 11 existing = 11
units.

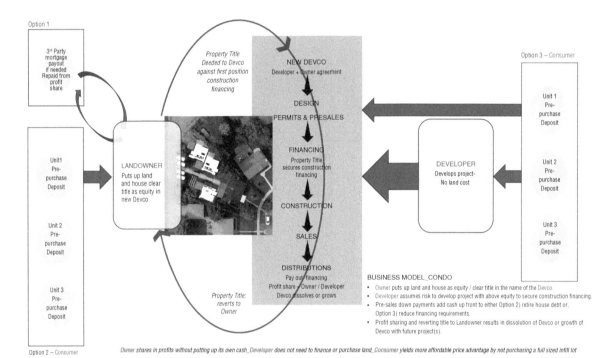

Option 1

3rd Party
mortgage
payout
if needed
Repaid from
profit
share

Property Title
Deeded to Devco
against first position
construction
financing

NEW DEVCO
Developer + Owner agreement

Option 3 – Consumer

Unit 1
Pre-
purchase
Deposit

DESIGN

PERMITS & PRESALES

Unit1
Pre-
purchase
Deposit

LANDOWNER
Puts up land
and house clear
title as equity in
new Devco

FINANCING
Property Title
secures construction
financing

DEVELOPER
Develops project-
No land cost

Unit 2
Pre-
purchase
Deposit

CONSTRUCTION

Unit 2
Pre-
purchase
Deposit

Unit 3
Pre-
purchase
Deposit

SALES

DISTRIBUTIONS
Pay out financing
Profit share + Owner / Developer
Devco dissolves or grows

Property Title:
reverts to
Owner

BUSINESS MODEL_CONDO
• Owner puts up land and house as equity / clear title in the name of the Devco.
• Developer assumes risk to develop project with above equity to secure construction financing.
• Pre-sales down payments add cash up front to either Option 2) retire house debt or,
  Option 3) reduce financing requirements.
• Profit sharing and reverting title to Landowner results in dissolution of Devco or growth of
  Devco with future project(s).

Unit 3
Pre-
purchase
Deposit

Option 2 – Consumer

Owner shares in profits without putting up its own cash_Developer does not need to finance or purchase land_Consumer yields more affordable price advantage by not purchasing a full sized infill lot

▲ Figure 4.1.5

Business Model—Condominium

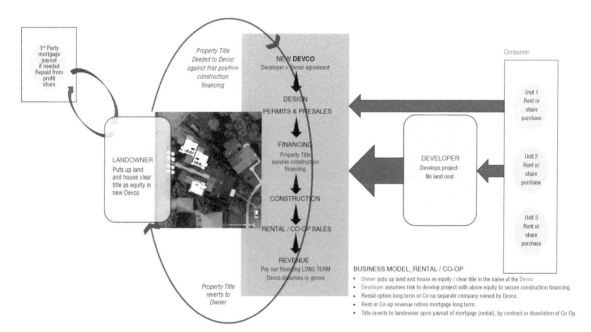

3rd Party mortgage payout if needed Repaid from profit share

Property Title Deeded to Devco against first position construction financing

NEW **DEVCO**
Developer + Owner agreement

Consumer

LANDOWNER
Puts up land and house clear title as equity in new Devco

DESIGN
PERMITS & PRESALES

FINANCING
Property Title secures construction financing

CONSTRUCTION

RENTAL / CO-OP SALES

REVENUE
Pay our financing LONG TERM
Devco dissolves or grows

Property Title reverts to Owner

DEVELOPER
Develops project-
No land cost

Unit 1
Rent or share purchase

Unit 2
Rent or share purchase

Unit 3
Rent or share purchase

BUSINESS MODEL_RENTAL / CO-OP

- Owner puts up land and house as equity / clear title in the name of the Devco.
- Developer assumes risk to develop project with above equity to secure construction financing.
- Rental option long term or Co-op separate company owned by Devco.
- Rent or Co-op revenue retires mortgage long term.
- Title reverts to landowner upon payout of mortgage (rental), by contract or dissolution of Co-Op.

Owner shares revenue without putting up its own cash_Developer does not need to finance or purchase land_Consumer yields more affordable price advantage

▲ Figure 4.1.6

Business Model—Rental/Co-op

The Business Model is discussed in detail in Chapter 4.2. Narrative: Business Model.

The costing information from the proforma in this narrative is included here (see Table 4.1.1) with a conservative illustration of the difference in cost between an infill and BAAKFIL unit on the same lot. For consistency, the same area and base building cost is used (excluding profit) for each example to emphasize the land cost impact.

	BAAKFIL	Infill
Demolition	0.00	30,000.00
Area	1600 sf	1600 sf
Cost / sf	208.62	208.62
Subtotal	333,789.00	363,789.00
Land allocation	21,333.00	350,000.00
TOTAL		
	$355,122.00	$713,789.00

◀ Table 4.1.1

Cost Comparison

The following matrix (see Table 4.1.2) summarizes considerations derived from the research with the business model that:

- promotes retention and reuse
- positions landowner as a partner/shareholder
- leverages landowner equity
- removes land cost from the developer proforma
- allows the landowner to age in community and retain tenure
- enables the development company to sell or rent
- increases affordability
- promotes respectful densification.

Red text in the matrix emphasizes areas where BAAKFIL innovations work to the benefit of the landowner, developer, consumer and community.

The research question is:

How can my practice deliver sustainable densification innovations that address attainability, affordability, demographics, bespoke needs and societal expectations, while being respectful to place?

The business model boldly and simply provides an answer to the research question:

Commit BAAKFIL

Chapter 4.2 Narrative: Business Model, goes further to explain the mechanics of the business model in a narrative format. This is an important analysis, evaluation and peer review of the *innovation of ways*, viewed through the eyes of the protagonists inside the business model—the banker, developer, landowner and consumer.

The narrative includes costing information and a development proforma. It explores alternate profitability scenarios and the veracity of the business model in various locations, the significant impact of the removal of land cost, and why. The narrative presents the case, asks and answers questions and probes the concerns particular to each protagonist.

I conclude this Chapter 4.1 with the following short survey of quotes from Key Informants KI*_9, the banker, KI_6, the non-profit developer and finally KI*_8, the for-profit developer:

> KI*_9 'We like the idea of a development company with the landowner as a partner The development company especially if it exists with a track record and has the land he wants to build on paid for already and it is put up as collateral; we can do business all the time'.
>
> KI_6 'Using the Community leagues to build credibility and serving a community by thinking about the socio-cultural make up of existing neighbourhoods is so important. People we talk to feel they are being pushed out'.
>
> KI*_8 'Related land costs (in Edmonton) range from $60,000 per unit in the suburbs to greater than $400,000 for a skinny lot in a desirable urban location. The average cost of a single family house in Edmonton is $462,000 in November 2021 and peaked at about $500,000 in mid 2022. It (Edmonton) is still one of the most economical places to buy a home … It is ironic that BAAKFIL is conceived here! … Units are definitely more affordable under this business model and achieve value by reducing the footprint and the cost of land …'

4.2 Narrative: Business Model

The mechanics of the business model introduced in Chapter 4.1 are described here in a detailed narrative that includes analysis, evaluation and peer review.

It is a compilation of data involving subject matter expert Key Informants who are formally interviewed and recorded at the beginning of the research and again at the end, when presented with the work and asked to review the output.

This results in a detailed technical analysis, evaluation and peer review of the *innovation of ways*, viewed through the eyes of

Matrix

COHORT	ISSUE	STRUCTURE	LEVERAGE

LANDOWNER	Owner needs to adjust:
	
	Age in community/downsize
	
	   Less maintenance
	
	   Adult children leaving
	
	   Aging parents need help
	
	BUT
	
	Lack of choice
	
	High cost to sell and buy again
		Existing mature neighbourhood
		
		   Bungalow or two storey
		
		   Pie Lot
		
		   Corner lot
		
		   50' lot
		
		Densification: need for right-size units and house renovations
			Existing property and equity as *consideration* – partnership position in new Devco
			
			   Equity position without cash
			
			   Cost effective development

DEVELOPMENT COMPANY (DEVCO)	Land acquisition now up to 50% cost of infill projects
	
	   Inflation
	
	   Interest rates
		Integrated business model
		
		   Developer
		
		   Owner
		
		   Investor or lender
		
		   (+ outsourced team as app)
			Land purchase not required
			
			Land cost removed
			
			Time and $$$ savings
			
			Financing burden reduced

CONSUMER	Land cost issues – attainability and affordability
	
	   Inflation
	
	   Interest rates
		Infill inherently structured to maximums
		
		   Cost
		
		   Size
		
		   Price
			No leverage with status quo

COMMUNITY	INFILL not serving intended purpose
	
	   High cost
	
	   Densification conflicts
	
	   Negative impacts - antipathy, fear
		Expectation of respect for neighbours and neighbourhood consultation
		
		   Scale and use
			Devco liaison with EFCL potentials
			
			   Consistent input and output
			
			   Representation on Devco Board?

CITY	Bylaws and Regulations
	
	   Inflexible to new demographics
	
	   Surcharge and fee increases
	
	   Mistrust
		Siloed administration
		
		   Lack of departmental integration
		
		   'Innovation constipation'
			New Bylaws pending
			
			   Timely opportunity
			
			   Demonstration (or Pilot project)

PROCESS	BENEFIT	OUTCOME
Silent partner or active client/user Outsourced professionals or 'in house' Owner has AGENCY Develop flexible, bespoke units on site with design Tool-kit. Remain as part of Devco or be bought out at any time after project completion.	Debt reduction or elimination Less risk / disruption Reduced maintenance Social equity / micro community Screen purchasers or renters Flexibility – sell or rent, short term or long term as shareholder	Increased property value and cash flow Sustainable property investment Support diversity, personal social contract(s) Flexible – adaptable Tool-kit Option to opt out or remain inside business model - other contracts / development options
Integrated Project Development (IPD) Devco does entire project Program, Proforma, Budgets Design, Financing, Construction Sales or Rent Project / Property Management	Units built / sold in less time Proportionate share of land (building footprint) sold only – similar to bare land condominium, reduced sale price. Market responsive to changing demographics with smaller units.	Scalable – mature urban neighbourhoods yield thousands of sites Sustainable Devco growth potential Neighbourhood context preserved Redefines infill Infrastructure improvements over time
CHOICE, flexibility with projects INCREASED affordability Alternate housing typologies Responsive to changing demographics / smaller units	Consumer access to right sized, more affordable mature neighbourhood housing without purchasing a full subdivided infill lot. **Land cost mitigated**	Increase availability to variable incomes and diverse urban cohort Affordable choices
Consultative Addresses NIMBY Demonstration Project Opportunity to reflect and evaluate	Devco as community advocate Neighbourhood character retained Builds trust Demonstration project proof of concept	Achieves ideals of 'gentle' urban neighbourhood densification Neighborhood context respected Addresses NIMBY
Demonstration project can be phased with Partial existing Bylaw compliance + new Bylaw flexibility	Demonstration project independent of policy Less risk for City Evaluation to test proof of concept	Positive influence on new Bylaws Broader acceptance / scalable Value added: increased tax revenue + neighbourhood acceptance

the protagonists inside the business model—the banker, developer, landowner and consumer.

The narrative includes costing information and a development proforma. It explores alternate scenarios to test the business model, the significant impact of the removal of land cost, and why.

It presents the case, asks and answers questions and probes the concerns particular to each protagonist. The narrative format is the mechanism that proves best suited for me to describe the results of organizing several similar inputs into a single voice.

Some comments can be jointly attributed to several individuals, given the complexity and over-lapping interests of Key Informants, CoP and my own synthesis of information generated from them.

Banker KI*_9
Developer KI_6 and KI*_8
Landowner (also KI_3)
Consumer KI*_11

Banker _ KI*_9

RESEARCHER: *I have presented the concept of the business model and I need you to summarise the criteria upon which this can fit within the financial products you sell. I have discussed the matter generally with independent mortgage lenders and private investors who each have their own thoughts about how this can work. Brokers have also told me that other sources such as pension fund managers and REIT's are anxious to become more connected with what I have learned is being referred to as longer term 'patient capital'. Each of these options poses different opportunities and risk to the developer. My hope is to test the model against a more conservative lender. You confirmed the necessary commodified nature of housing product in the building industry in our first meeting. The need for banks to do their due diligence in basically eliminating risk is understood; therefore predictable re-sellable product is easier to support in case of default, than that of bespoke design. Not good news to architects but to be clear, if the merits of the business model can be supported within the regulated banking industry, then I know there are other financing options for proof of concept that can also be pursued.*

BANKER _ KI*_9: This is a very different approach to development and an interesting idea. Specifically, the prospect is interesting from the first time buyer I assume all the way up to elder care. The cost is less than infill and an owner can monetize its asset. That said, the look can be more affordable or wildly expensive. Based on what I do, the basic questions you first need to answer to work with our funding models are:

Who is the beneficiary?

Who is to benefit?

Does zoning support this legally?

For us to consider financing any new real estate product development, the original house on a site must be free and clear; no debt or encumbrance. Maybe the developer can help with a separate private deal here if needed; but for any loan instrument you must get rid of debt first. Any registrations on the land must also be cleared. We will require a first position mortgage; otherwise in case of a foreclosure, we'd be left with nothing.

RESEARCHER: *What if the landowner does not own the property outright and there is a mortgage in place, even with another institution?*

BANKER _ KI*_9: We need clear title on the property. We could do an appraisal and re-finance the property to the owner, but this would be a separate transaction. Is this still being done with the owner as a partner in a development company?

RESEARCHER: *Yes, so if I understand it right—since the Devco is the borrower and if the owner puts up the land to the Devco and the landowner borrows separately to clear the residual debt against the property, then the property can be put into the Devco clear title?*

BANKER _ KI*_9: Yes. As I said we need to have clear title on the property. If the owner is able to pay out the mortgage on the property with a line of credit or whatever instrument, then the property is paid for and the property can be put up free and clear to the development company. The owner still has a debt to pay to whomever, but that debt cannot be pledged against the land. In other words whether it is us or someone else who does this, the clear title is key. The owner takes the risk, we don't.

RESEARCHER: *So then when the property is developed by the Devco, the units are sold and the landowner gets his share of the profit, he can do with that what he wishes including paying out any third party debt if any?*

BANKER _ KI*_9: Yes. It is cleaner to start debt free. One obvious option is for the landowner to arrange separate financing before coming to us with this model. Say for example the landowner gets his or her parents to cover the debt and the landowner works out a private repayment plan with the parents. We see this more and more with parents doing this to increase down payments to help their children qualify to enter the market for new product. It is basically the same idea. We just need to have the property free and clear against a construction loan or long-term financing.

We won't take the risk otherwise.

We like the idea of a development company with the landowner as a partner. The development company especially if it exists with a track record and has the land he wants to build on paid for already and it is put up as collateral; we can do business all the time.

However the company is structured and profit shared is not up to us. We just need to protect the loan against the asset. This is an equitable deal for the landowner too because the developer is assuming risk alongside the owner with the land. It is being transferred to the development company, even temporarily, and the legal agreement between the owner and the developer would address these things so the landowner is protected too. Obviously the landowner is gambling his equity, but if the deal is a good one the risks are still less than developments where the land is not already owned.

Again, the banks are not interested in anything other than securing the loan in whatever form it takes. Developers know all this. We still need to review their statements, net worth and such things and be comforttable they are solvent. They may need to put up some equity too but not having to buy or finance land puts them in a great spot to start though.

Regardless of third party financing or not, is there a way for the landowner to recoup his investment quickly upon sales?

BANKER _ KI*_9: I take this to mean if there is more than one unit? Sure, we do partial discharges on properties if the units are on separate land titles. A condo typically is one titled property, however. If there are separate titles remember we want in on all of them. That may not be the case with a condominium where there is one title and common property. In that sense all units would need to be sold unless there was some way to pay out the loan sooner. Then you can do whatever you want.

RESEARCHER: *OK how do you see a rental scenario? I have actually been asked by one of my Key Informants to consider this as well as a condo model in the business plan. I learned he is considering BAAKFIL on his property with his son and family.*

BANKER _ KI*_9: Same criteria; debt free, doable but more difficult. Rental is more 'on spec'. A financed rental apartment is always tougher and is a reason why developers take the path of least resistance—away from it, unless there is a strong market demand. We'd need to see the cash flow proforma. A condo just needs to be sold—in and out quicker, much easier for the bank to evaluate.

Rental project criteria varies, a lot. How is the debt going to be paid over 25–30 years? What are the forecasted rents and expenses over a 12-month period; extended over the length of time of the mortgage? Do they square with the market? How much equity is placed to reduce the risk? It is done all the time but is more challenging because the banks are more demanding. We look at neutral revenue streams first—understanding the costs—so then we can determine the workability and margins. Other lenders of course as you may know, may see this differently and be willing to absorb more risk.

RESEARCHER: *Any comments on the preliminary proforma that I sent you? It is based on a project we did with a developer who is part of my community of practice—a client who is interested in this model.*

BANKER _ KI*_9: I think it was a bit light at the start but it was adjusted. It generally costs more to build fewer units in the city centre than more units on the outskirts but that is just my own view based on volume transactions.

Servicing costs can be higher for infill in the older neighbourhoods and the City is always charging more to redo things like streets, sidewalks, sewers. The City always forces it to be much more costly.

Your costs per square foot of sales in Edmonton at $250+ seem to be in the correct range for mid to higher level product in the market today (2021–2022). High end custom infill on the other hand can be much, much more at $400–$500/sf as I expect you know.

RESEARCHER: *Any final thoughts?*

BANKER _ KI*_9: To reiterate, first position mortgage over the land is key to doing business with us. Move the title to the development company and get the landowner off the title. Let your legal people deal with disposition and re-position of the land ownership if I understand it right, after all is done. I would recommend your proforma include a contingency for the cost overruns that always seem to appear. And recourse—someone always points fingers.

Depending on the partnership, personal guarantees might be needed but not always depending on the capitalization and liquidity of the development company.

All things considered, this would be the right way approach, supportable under our normal course of business if the partnership is sound. The banks will buy in if the partners buy in.

The market is the final arbiter. The first deals are the toughest. A 75% loan for the first project is aggressive to start—60–65% is probably more realistic. That's just the bank. When the market shows it works, that can change.

Developer _ KI*_8

RESEARCHER: *Let's visit the proforma process.*

DEVELOPER KI*_8: This pie lot proposal incorporates a new business model where the cost of land is leveraged by the property owner who, in an equity partnership with the developer, puts up the land in the back of the property for development, making it available to the developer at $0.00. In addition, land cost is mitigated to the consumer by the sale of only the proportionate value of the land footprint occupied by each individual unit. The landowner remains in place in the existing house to age in community while sharing in the profit from sales of new units or the cash flow generated if a rental option is pursued.

When you and I first talked, we discussed using our Missing Middle Design competition entry back in 2019 as a start point. You recall we struggled to get the numbers to work for mixed use, intergenerational, net zero ready townhouse lofts and a small café, because the City had a fixed price for the land and obligated everyone to put the five lots they owned in at $1,700,000.

This was $600,000 over the assessment value at the time, so it was aggressive market pricing when considering the average value of a lot in Spruce Avenue at the time was slightly under $250,000. The appraised values were much less on the two smaller vacant lots too. There was a burden of $81,000 per unit before you even started design. Larger projects and higher density would have helped of course, but you decided, actually we both decided, given the mature neighbourhood and the market, to stay with a bare land condominium. As it happened, it took four years for the City to get a project going. (Not sure what they have done yet either). If the City had partnered with us by putting the land in at $0.00 they would have gotten fair value out for the land by now and we could have completed the work in about 16 months. They only just demolished the site in February 2023.

RESEARCHER: *Are you saying that the business model can work with municipal owned land as well as with privately owned land?*

DEVELOPER KI*_8: Conceptually speaking yes of course it can. Why not? Now, we all know the City has a land bank and their Real Estate Department is its own profit centre, so they do drive up land prices—even for the vacant infill lots they sell. They are always over market plus these are usually properties in areas where the house needs to be torn down, if it hasn't been already and the developer has to pay for improvement levies such as new sidewalks, fire hydrants, sewers, even paving lanes, in addition to the usual utility connection fees.

It is onerous but the model itself can still easily work if someone could convince the City to test it. For the design competition, we needed time to line up short-term financing in the event we had won, given the really tight schedule provided. If we could have removed the $1.7m, it would have been so much easier and the project would have cost $6m instead of $8m. With the land, the soft costs were almost 40% of the project.

RESEARCHER: *So this is reflected in the final sales proforma if I remember right?*

DEVELOPER KI*_8: Yes, but not accurately. We couldn't pass this on to the market for more than $225/sf averaged at the time because higher price absorption in that older neighbourhood just wasn't there. Project risk usually means we should target 25–30% profit as we always know it ends up being less. Selling at around $480,000–$500,000 per unit, while lower than infill, was pushing the upper limit already. We had a cost base of $7.834m against forecasted sales of $9.252m for profit of about $65,000/unit. That is only a 17% margin. If the land had been at $0.00, the city could have seen a decent return and we could have sold for more like $400,000 and still do better than 17%. Greed and land cost are intermingled because land is always priced to what the market will bear. As you know, it isn't real cost, it is a fabricated cost.

RESEARCHER: *OK. What about the pie lot project?*

DEVELOPER KI*_8: You and I have pro-rated the Missing Middle proforma to vet it regularly over the past two years. Your units do vary more in size, 600sf–1200sf (56sm–112sm) for the smaller units to 1700sf (160sm) for the large units over three levels with a rental suite option, all without a basement. We don't need basements anymore.

Even with the smaller units, it is fair to assume that competing build types are suburban townhomes, infill duplexes, triplexes or single family 'skinny' homes. While many of these build types are bigger, the cost of land is still the single largest factor in each case. Typical competing sell prices in 2021–2022 range from a low of $360,000 for suburban townhomes to $1,000,000 or more for infill 'skinny' homes in desirable neighbourhoods. Related land costs range from $60,000 per unit in the suburbs to greater than $400,000 for a skinny lot in a desirable, urban location. The average cost of a single family house in Edmonton is $462,000 per November 2021 and peaked at about $500,000 in mid 2022.

BAAKFIL units are designed with an option for lower level suites. If rented, the selling price is achievable for a broader demographic. Example: A mortgage payment at of $2300 per month and net rental income of $700 per month, for many years with low interest rates would reduce income to qualify from $7700 per month to $5375 per month. The largest units provide up to three bedrooms and a work loft over three levels but the footprint is no larger than a 24 x 24 double car garage.

Units are definitely more affordable under this business model and achieve value by reducing the building footprint and the cost of land, yet can still achieve the upper end of comparable living space with a finished lower level. I know you want to trend to smaller units, but they are nevertheless parcelled as bare land condominium units, with a common yard shared with the existing homeowner.

Suburban townhomes in Edmonton are typically in the 1200–1600 SF range (plus basement). Example: A mortgage payment of $1400 per month makes these units competitive with rental apartments of the same size, even after factoring in homeowner association fees, utilities, common area maintenance, insurance and property taxes.

Your specifications are comparable with the market. Pushing the sustainability agenda to achieve net zero can add 3–5% to the cost. Services like hot water can in some cases be supplied from a centrally located high efficiency condensing boiler or on-demand tankless systems. In-floor radiant heating is a great primary heat source with individual energy recovery ventilators (ERVs or HRVs) to provide exhaust and fresh air exchange. This is more cost efficient than separately metered and individual heating, ventilation and air conditioning (HVAC) units. Your geothermal systems and geo-piles, earth tube AC and high-performance envelope standards such as triple glazing, higher R values, etc., all contribute to that sustainability agenda. The building envelope

Proforma

BAAKFIL Proforma			01-Mar-19	01-Jan-23	01-Jan-23
			Missing Middle	Proforma	Proforma
Mar-23			21 Unit s	Single Unit Analysis	Three Unit Analysis
1	Consultant fees, Survey	3.3%	165,000.00	8,991.00	26,973.00
2	Permits	1.1%	53,500.00	2,915.00	8,745.00
3	Site Services	2.3%	116,000.00	6,321.00	18,963.00
4	Foundation Excavation, Hourly Equipment	1.6%	77,500.00	4,223.00	12,669.00
5	Concrete Work	8.9%	445,000.00	24,251.00	72,753.00
6	Framing	12.4%	617,000.00	33,624.00	100,872.00
7	Roofing	2.0%	101,000.00	5,504.00	16,512.00
8	Windows and Doors	2.6%	130,000.00	7,084.00	21,252.00
9	Exterior finishing	9.7%	483,000.00	26,322.00	78,966.00
10	Masonry	1.0%	49,500.00	2,697.00	8,091.00
11	Electrical	5.8%	291,500.00	15,885.00	47,655.00
12	Plumbing, Heating, Sprinklers	12.9%	644,000.00	35,095.00	105,285.00
13	Elevators	0.0%	0.00	-	-
14	Insulation & Drywall	9.0%	447,000.00	24,360.00	73,080.00
15	Painting	2.3%	117,000.00	6,376.00	19,128.00
16	Interior finishing, Cabinets, Appliances	9.1%	455,000.00	24,796.00	74,388.00
17	Floor coverings incl. Tiles	3.3%	165,000.00	8,990.00	26,970.00
18	Landscaping, Paving & Fencing	2.8%	137,500.00	7,493.00	22,479.00
19	Cleaning	0.8%	42,000.00	2,289.00	6,867.00
20	Supervision & Casual Labour	2.8%	140,000.00	7,628.00	22,884.00
21	Security	1.2%	60,000.00	3,271.00	9,813.00
22	Site General Expenses	1.0%	49,000.00	2,671.00	8,013.00
23	Insurance	1.2%	58,000.00	3,160.00	9,480.00
24	Service & Warranty (2yr Labour & Materials)	0.4%	21,000.00	1,145.00	3,435.00
25	New Home Warranty	0.3%	12,500.00	680.00	2,040.00
26	Legal	0.6%	31,000.00	1,689.00	5,067.00
27	Marketing	1.7%	84,000.00	4,577.00	13,731.00
	Building Costs	100.0%	$ 4,992,000.00	$ 272,037.00	$ 816,111.00

#	Description		Col1	Col2	Col3
28	Contingency @ 5%		250,000.00	13,602.00	40,848.00
29	Admin./Mgmt 8% Bldg Cost		400,000.00	21,763.00	65,357.00
30	Selling Commissions		207,000.00	10,881.00	32,678.00
31	Financing/Property Taxes		285,500.00	15,506.00	46,566.00
32	Land		**1,700,000.00**	**0.00**	**0.00**
	Soft Costs		**$ 2,842,500.00**	**$ 61,752.00**	**$ 185,449.00**
	Total Costs		**$ 7,834,500.00**	**$ 333,789.00**	**$ 1,001,560.00**
	$/sf cost average 1600SF each unit		220.00 - 233.17	$ 208.62	$ 208.62
	Sales				
	Subtotal			**333,789.00**	**1,001,560.00**
	Land allocation 1800SF/10,876sf = 16%				
	Assessment 2023 @ 336,000 say 400,000 MV			21,333.00	64,000.00
	Total with land allocation			**355,122.00**	**1,065,560.00**
	Sales price – profit @ 15% = 53,268 _ 159,834		255.24 / sf	**$ 408,390.00**	$ 1,225,394.00
	Sales price – profit @ 20% = 71,024 _ 213,112		266.34 / sf	**$ 426,146.00**	$ 1,278,672.00
	Sales price – profit @ 25% = 88,780 _ 266,390		277.44 / sf	**$ 443,902.00**	$ 1,331,950.00
	Sales price – profit @ 30% = 106,536 _ 319,668		288.54 / sf	**$ 461,658.00**	$ 1,385,228.00

must meet or exceed the 2020 National Energy Code for Buildings (NECB) including R80 roofs and a minimum of R40 walls.

Using durable exterior cementitious or metal panels, non-combustible is good. Preparing south facing roofs for photovoltaic solar panels is good. Collect rainwater in cistern(s) for irrigation, gardening, car washing and recycle grey water for toilet flushing. The project can become net zero or beyond net zero if sharing self-generated on-site energy, depending upon market forces and price points. Sharing energy supply on-site— this goes to your idea of the one minute city does it not?

Proforma 2

Profit Share	1 Unit Landowner 37.5%	3 Units Landowner 37.5%	1 Unit Developer 62.5%	3 Units Developer 62.5%
Sales price – profit @ 15% = 53,268 _ 159,834	$ 408,390.00	$ 1,225,394.00	$ 408,390.00	$ 1,225,394.00
Sales price – profit @ 20% = 71,024 _ 213,112	$ 426,146.00	$ 1,278,672.00	$ 426,146.00	$ 1,278,672.00
Sales price – profit @ 25% = 88,780 _ 266,390	$ 443,902.00	$ 1,331,950.00	$ 443,902.00	$ 1,331,950.00
Sales price - profit @ 30% = 106,536 _ 319,668	$ 461,658.00	$ 1,385,228.00	$ 461,658.00	$ 1,385,228.00
	$19,975.00	$59,937.00	$33,293.00	$99,897.00
	$26,634.00	$79,917.00	$44,390.00	$133,195.00
	$33,292.00	$99,896.00	$55,488.00	$166,494.00
	$39,951.00	$119,875.00	$66,585.00	$199,793.00

Finishes aligning with new condominiums—painted drywall, plank flooring, porcelain tile, quartz countertops and component storage cupboard installations all make sense.

An option to sell the building shell with interior finishes completed by the owner could further reduce the sale price by 15% or more and we can talk about that more.

Cost estimates use the same specification for finishes and building technology; for up to three units on your pie lot [Chapter 6.1 Demonstration Projects] in Q4 2022 dollars. Goods and Services Tax (GST) and upgrading to the house is not included.

RESEARCHER: *Yes, we pro-rated the initial estimates prepared in 2019 on much more detailed drawings and the similarities in construction specifications, which were consistent with BAAKFIL to begin with. The figures were updated in 2021 and 2022 for BAAKFIL by a 14% increase, representing modest increases in 2020 and 2021 and a full 10% increase in 2022. Inflation and interest rates surged in Q4 of 2022 and show signs of moderation in early 2023.*

In order to maintain consistency year over year for reporting purposes and to ensure an 'apples to apples' comparison from 2019 to Q1 of 2023, the current inflation and interest rate picture in Canada is not factored in as an anomaly despite its impact; to not skew the numbers.

Everyone is affected by this, so it is all relative anyway. Estimates are also consistent with the feedback up to Q1 2023 when the research was deemed complete.

Mortgage calculations are based on prior year's average rates of around 5.65% with a CMHC minimum 5% DP and 25 year amortization, also consistent with conditions prior to the inflation surge in 2022. Affordability is based on the CMHC standard metric of 30% of gross income to qualify.

Sales prices are set at variable profit margins, to allow for location and the different average financial market strength in mature neighbourhoods. The demonstration pie lot pilot project for which this estimate is based is more suited to the 15%–20% profit profile.

Sales prices also fit the market compared with assessments and tax data per the City of Edmonton.

The Missing Middle proforma also targeted sales prices of $222/sf to a high of $268/sf depending upon unit size in a neighbourhood not unlike the pie lot pilot project. Units were priced from $290,000 for a small 1080sf unit to $548,000 for a 2160sf unit with 'granny' suite. Average cost was $480,000 for a 1600sf unit compared to about $455,000 for a single family house in the city at the time. This included a land component of $81,000 per unit (averaged) with the requirement for the $1,700,000 land component.

With the land at $0.00, the pie lot BAAKFIL units that average 1600sf are significantly less, from $408,390 to $426,146 with profit margins at 15–20%. This margin in this particular mature neighbourhood is deemed healthy given the savings in time and money relative to the land procurement component.

DEVELOPER KI*_8: It is interesting that the BAAKFIL costs today are still similar to the average price of properties in the area and well below the average cost of a single family home in Edmonton. The other comparable is of course the cost of infill, which in the wealthier central areas is $750,000 to over a million dollars. Starting prices for the small townhomes at Blatchford are priced from $490,000 to $600,000.

The other thing of course is these prices are based on an average of 1600sf/unit. Some are larger and others are smaller. Your universal unit would likely be priced in the $390,000 range.

Removing the land cost makes a big difference.

RESEARCHER: *What other observations can you offer about the building industry?*

DEVELOPER KI*_8: Do you mean as it relates to BAAKFIL?

RESEARCHER: *Yes please.*

DEVELOPER KI*_8: Well these may seem like random points but you will recognize they are core values for our company and come from completing hundreds of multi-storey condo and apartment units.

Currently in Edmonton roughly 50% is construction cost, 25% soft costs in the broadest sense (design, approvals, marketing, financing etc. etc.) and 25% land cost. It varies but this is rule of thumb today.

Developers always try to reduce the land component by increasing density. In the suburbs the land component can be as low as $15,000 per door (less than 10% of the unit value); however, on the other hand, land for a duplex in the University area sits at $250,000 per door (likely 40–50% of the unit value), with everything else somewhere in between.

Rising interest rates and inflation in late 2022 affect the 'soft' cost component, not only for construction financing, but also risk. Approval delays, construction delays, occupancy delays are all compounded in a high interest rate environment.

Developer margins, I believe need to be in the 20–30% range based on our current development methodologies but these get squeezed during recessions or inflationary times (developers typically absorb price increases during construction). However, these are only short-term occurrences and will eventually revert to a new norm.

Unless new construction methods are developed, construction costs, i.e. labour and materials are very much market driven. The industry is competitive, so arguably there is not a lot of room to change construction costs dramatically without some new disruptive technology introduced. The house building industry is very unsophisticated and unskilled so disruptive technologies—that many claim as progress—is rarely found in the house building industry. For example, I'd use insulated concrete forms (ICFs) and structural insulated panel systems (SIPS) all the time instead of traditional cribbing and wall framing, but it is hard to break those product lines into the marketplace despite their big advantages. We are a long way from your desire for 3D printing, mass timber, even prefabrication in bulk.

Land cost, if urban sprawl is allowed to continue unabated can and will stay relatively low relative to overall inflation on the periphery of cities, but not in the middle. However, huge infrastructure costs need to be accounted for through property taxes or other government sources. This is beside the costs of dealing with decaying city cores and the social impacts. Land is still the issue regardless.

In Toronto, Vancouver or Osaka, Japan where I once lived, land is three times the cost of the housing unit. Toronto and Vancouver have largely run out of suburban land and have hugely greater land component costs for housing compared to Edmonton which is still one of the most economical places to buy a home in the country.

It is ironic that BAAKFIL is conceived here!

All this obviously leads me to state that any way land cost can be taken out of the formulae for any kind of housing model is a big win for developers. Risk and uncertainty is reduced. Lower margins by not being able to mark up land notwithstanding; less risk means that actual profitability can be more accurately forecast and, with the time saved, we can not only do more projects, but we can bring them to market for less.

So BAAKFIL from that perspective makes sense.

Now to the earlier question about why condominiums do not go up in value (price) the same as housing on titled lots. This is a consideration for BAAKFIL. In a multi-unit condo building the cost is mostly for the structure, a smaller portion for the land. However, when selling in the future, the building has depreciated, so there is no value in the land component because nothing further can be done with it. Hence, prices of condos are pretty much stagnant, actually going down when inflation is factored in.

Compare this with a typical 60-year-old house on a lot in Edmonton—your pie lot for example. Realistically the house is worthless, however it is still worth say $400,000 or more because of land value. The gain in owning a home on a titled lot is usually related to the land value, not the structure. This is usually how we justify infill. Tear down a worthless house, subdivide and maximize the land value for sale. (Value in re-useable material goes to waste, sure, but that is a different story and few in the industry really care about that yet).

So, where am I going with this? If the land can be separated from the structure, something akin to building on leased land, then opportunities can be created. First, financing could change and CMHC could drive this. Financing for land should be at the lowest rate possible. The land is not going anywhere, does not depreciate and will increase in value. At least it keeps up with inflation and the cost of developing greenfield land. It is logical the financing cost should reflect this. If land is financed at a really low rate and longer term (why not 50 years) and only the structure is financed at market rates, then financing home ownership could be reduced significantly, especially for infill, e.g. high land value developments.

Finally, the topic close to your heart is the potential through infill, of BAAKFIL.

The undeveloped portion of an existing residential property is like free land.

The analogy can be to a commercial property. If you have a 40,000sf shop on a 400,000sf site do you consider the land value when contemplating an expansion? Likely not, you simply assess the cost of the addition or new building when deciding to expand. This exact same concept can and maybe should apply to residential properties.

Thinking about the idea this way makes it a lot easier to understand how important removing land cost can be from the house building equation. The fact that you keep the existing house also fits. You are just doing another form of expansion. It also seems a pretty strong way to convince a neighbourhood or a community (by not doing any demolition) that you are setting up to be a good neighbour.

Developer 2_KI_6

RESEARCHER: *Thank you for helping me seek additional perspective within the development community beyond the typical profit oriented model. As a non-profit developer, how do you see the aspirations and interventions of BAAKFIL impacting your business?*

DEVELOPER KI 6: I find that whenever we are working in an older neighbourhood, we always come up against those who are so in love with their house—their home—that the first thing they think about is how it will be negatively impacted by me, the developer. I am always reminded that one's biggest private investment is most often their house so it is natural to want to protect it and any personal interests as well.

As a non-profit, we see this especially with working class people who have something they have worked hard to obtain and will fight to hold on to their property all the time. The City still has trouble understanding this.

BAAKFIL as a name and acronym as an idea is spot on. We don't need to build huge housing. Using the Community Leagues to build credibility and serving a community by thinking about the socio-cultural make-up of existing neighbourhoods is so important. People we talk to feel they are being pushed out. I want to give them confidence in our projects that we aren't trying to do that and our low-cost micro prefab units are only one example. Cities are really struggling to think differently about affordability and the social aspects of communities that are being atomized by displacement. Infill is not the answer. I support the idea of not disrupting the fabric of a neighbourhood. This is important since most cities have not reckoned with the scale of change needed.

But why must we do high, high density all the time? Look at parts of Montreal. I love the plex units you told me about.

We need more people thinking about how to do these types of housing projects and create a mechanism where many different options can be pursued.

So, I think about BAAKFIL as it asks a lot of the right questions and I think that its potential could be more far-reaching than you expect. Jane Jacobs wrote that the suburbs will repair themselves over time. Couldn't BAAKFIL work here too?

RESEARCHER: *Well that might be for some other DDes candidate to explore. I focus on the mature urban neighbourhood; but I do see the potential of this as a Pan-Canadian idea. Many cities have back alleys, residual underutilized land in mature neighbourhoods and all our cities face attainability and affordability issues.*

DEVELOPER KI_6: Affordability is the key and your idea of removing the land cost is pivotal. As a non-profit, I cannot afford high land cost because the numbers won't work. It takes too long to assemble anyway. I have to rely on angel investors who are willing to go long term, but they command more than the banks so it is not sustainable as a business model. Philanthropists have donated land to help a cause they believe in, but that is not a system.

My non-profit work is mostly rental. Basically I have to sell out before everything is paid off. I have a for-profit operation too and it subsidizes my non-profit community development company, so I can still make a living.

In my projects, I pay myself 5% of construction cost as a management fee to live and then I just carefully curate my tenants who pay just enough rent so the rental revenue calculations are satisfied. This is always less than market rents, 80%, sometimes lower. That's the rental model as a non-profit landlord.

When it comes to the sale of units at below market prices, my First-Right-of-Refusal on a buyback at the original price is what is emphasized when selling the unit. The unit is not an investment vehicle, it is a living space. Buy back at the original price means I can resell it with the same conditions and 'presto' I have perpetual affordability in a home ownership model. The issue with below market sales, however, is we find the first buyer always cashes out and the unit goes back up to market prices and passes on market value escalation immediately to the next buyer. That is why either a buy-back clause or a co-op model is what I'm pursuing.

Your BAAKFIL proforma calculations show a range of profit margins and you have asked me what is appropriate in my world. If 25% still proves the point of affordability and keeps the landowner satisfied, then win! Investors who have bought land for me have often said that 15% is fantastic, so 25% would be a no-brainer. And I am paying them out at 20% per year. In a co-op, which is a community on its own, this can be addressed by the cohort itself looking for stability in a mature neighbourhood and their own concepts of affordability. If they were to sell and make 30% or more, where are they going to go? That kind of clout is from decades of 30% margins from land holdings that I brokered when I worked for a large developer.

A 30% profit margin is still seen as respecttable. But is this world changing? The last house I built with a contractor in the Highlands cost us $600,000 all in, and we put it on the market at the wrong time as the market was going soft. Instead of $800,000, at a 30% mark up, it eventually sold a year later for $649,000. That's when I joined the City and started on my journey to get educated about housing needs in Edmonton which has led to my non-profit community development company today.

When I started out, new subdivision lots were $35,000. A walkout pie lot backing onto a huge irrigation pond was $100,000, which at the time was the threshold of sell-ability in Edmonton. Starter houses then had to be under $200,000 and the profit margin on those was 10% and everyone made money. At these rates, the partner companies we dealt with in subdivision building—I worked in the land division for three years—were turning over one house a day. Another large group could put up a house in four weeks. Times changed.

So my point on profit is that smaller units and more partners, such as a landowner, changes the entire mix. The landowner is getting to monetize his property and the development company assumes just about all of the risk. But the development company gets to build in less time (all things considered about zoning, permits, etc.) without buying land.

Because there is always risk, I would have to say the bottom line for developers of all types still has to be a profit margin built in that exceeds what can be expected to be earned with other much safer instruments through investment houses or in the markets. Otherwise why bother? We have learned this the hard way. This would begin at 15% based on your proforma and this would likely stand the test for a small, efficiently executed project. By mitigating the cost of land to the consumer, the housing is still more affordable. Therefore, the question should always be, what is fair to all parties and how will price points be met in the marketplace?

It does seem that the range still has to be between 15% and 30% in the industry. The market will absolutely tell you what metric will work best in certain areas, depending upon the community.

RESEARCHER: *This is a wonderful point and counterpoint discussion between developers. Any final thoughts?*

DEVELOPER KI_6: I would like to figure out a way to try a BAAKFIL project someday. It fits our business criteria for densification and affordability.

Landowner/also KI_3

RESEARCHER: *We have had many discussions about BAAKFIL now for about a year. Your house is clear title on a corner lot with lane access on two sides, with the LRT Valley Line expansion set to open nearby, within easy walking distance. You will have as you've said, a lesser need for your car and thus have good reason to stay in the neighbourhood.*

You are trying to imagine BAAKFIL to include one or possibly two units, with individual rental suites (four units in two buildings) with one unit for your son and small family. I know you have more questions since we first started these discussions and since the business model is fully vetted with the bank now, I can better address the uncertain areas from before.

LANDOWNER/ ALSO KI_3: The big question we still have relates to the partnership formula. You told me that the property owner contributes its equity to the development company that is formed for the BAAKFIL project. The property owner also contributes the land, which is obviously a key part of the endeavour. How is the land contribution valued in your equation? Does the property owner's share of the development company reflect the value of the land being contributed in addition to whatever equity the property owner puts in?

RESEARCHER: *I started into the business model proposition with the notion of the homeowner's equity being a flexible amount; so the landowner could vary its contribution relative to the value of the property, the size of the project and the amount of risk willing to be taken. I have since met with banking officials, as well with two developer/builders (one a client), to further develop the business model and a generic budget proforma.*

While the initial idea is negotiable with some developers and private investors, my conclusion is to make the model acceptable to the regulated banking industry first. Then there is certainty that it could work with other less risk-averse parties (using their own legal counsel as well). So, with this strategy I am now testing two scenarios—one where there is actually debt against the property and another where there is clear title such as your situation.

To simplify the financing approval process, the bank requires the entire property—house and land—be put up as clear title in the name of the new Devco. The developer may need to provide equity as well, depending on the total cost of the construction and the amount financed.

This is the simplest way to secure traditional construction financing where the bank takes first position on the security—loan or mortgage.

However, the process is cyclical since title is returned to the original landowner (original house and residual land) after the construction is completed, the new units are sold and the construction financing debt is paid out.

This effectively negates the idea of using partial equity, at least with the banks, for now.

There are three derivative ways that I have designed, however, to enable this to proceed.

1) A third party engages the landowner to pay out any remaining mortgage so the property can be transferred clear title. This can be done through an investor, parental loans, or a separate secure or unsecured line of credit.

2) It may be less desirable to the developer but still possible for the landowner to secure early deposits from purchasers to pay out the mortgage. This can work if the landowner already has a targeted clientele such as family or friends or colleagues. The deposits used to pay out the mortgage would be credited against your share of proceeds from sales by the Devco.

3) If the property is already clear title, then it follows the same path—title changes to the Devco.

This reduces the amount of financing required to be secured by the Devco and takes the cost of land entirely out of the developer project cost burden.

Pre-sales and deposit receipts into the Devco directly, also leverages the required project financing amounts. Every lender responds to sales already under contract. This is not only similar to the housing industry pre-sales process, but this gives important agency to the landowner as a partner in the Devco, who may wish to have a direct say in who the units are sold to (family, colleagues, etc).

This equity contribution means the landowner holds a larger percentage in the Devco and earns a larger return. In the case of the pie lot with three units, basically a $1m project the owner would have about a 40% interest in the Devco and proportionate return on sales. In your case, with two new units instead of three, the percentage would be higher based on the same rates.

LANDOWNER/ ALSO KI_3: RESEARCHER: How is the equity calculated?

Banks usually trigger an appraisal, make comparisons with the market, examine other data such as city property tax assessments and come up with a number. It is generally less than market value. This would be identified and signed off by all parties, presumably as a condition of the partnership.

If we use the Edmonton average cost of $500,000 as your equity in the property, the banks would likely come in lower at around 80% or say $400,000. If we were to develop two units on your lot, that could represent a range of about a 50%–60% share in the Devco depending on the total budget for the project. At a cost of say $700,000 and sales at $860,000, the profit would be somewhere around $160,000 and your share is at least half of that. That is a healthy return in just over a year if everything is sold. Remember you do not have to invest any cash. This is precisely how you monetize your property while still living in it.

In a sale situation, once everything is closed out, the house reverts back to you again.

LANDOWNER/
ALSO KI_3:

How does this square up with the supply chain uncertainty and construction costs?

RESEARCHER:

Yes, with inflation, interest rate increases and supply chain issues over the past year, costs are not easy to predict. With the uncertainty of Covid, we have seen 2x4 studs at $10 each and softwood plywood at $100 per sheet, but we also know this is not long term. Despite inflation, these things are beginning to moderate including the average cost of a single family home. It has come down a little with interest rate increases to stem the inflation tide.

New product on the outskirts is still more, on smaller lots even, but it is still possible— depending upon size and quality—to sell for less in this business model. It is all relative when land cost is removed.

Based on my conversations, with inflation, construction costs vary all over depending who you talk to. Right now, the banking industry input suggests using $250/sf. One developer I am working with is using $175/sf. In addition to what I just mentioned, this is still impacted by construction quality—materials, products and finishes, labour, developer buying power, soft costs like city connection charges, fees and improvement levies. I wish it could be more scientific but that is the industry we live in.

LANDOWNER/
ALSO KI_3:

Understood. OK, I just want to be really clear here, back to the clear title requirement. When

	you refer to the property owner giving clear title to the Devco, the owner becomes part of that company, correct?
RESEARCHER:	*Yes*
LANDOWNER/ ALSO KI_3:	So during construction, the company of which the property owner is a part—the Devco—owns the property. So for a time, the Devco of which we are a part would own the property on which we live (presumably not charging us rent) and then after construction, we get back clear title when new units are sold and files close with the bank.
RESEARCHER:	*Again, yes although technically the bank still has first call against the property if the project fails and it needs to foreclose. This is a remote possibility of course but that is how traditional financing fits with the banks, mortgage loans or other instruments.*
LANDOWNER/ ALSO KI_3:	Understood. Now I can see how that works in a condo model, but how would that work if the plan was to just rent out the new units? Is there a way for the Devco to own the rental units and the property owner to own the original house where there isn't a subdivision?
RESEARCHER:	*Good question. A rental situation is quite different and this can get complicated but rental scenarios still work with BAAKFIL. It first depends upon whether you wish to remain in the Devco.*

Generally in a rental situation, bankers have clearly said to me they need to be satisfied that the construction financing (that would likely be converted into a longer term mortgage), can be retired over time on the basis of a cash flow proforma relative to the new rental units only, because only the new units are financed. The new units, if rented, would end up being the collateral on the mortgage held by the bank with the Devco as the mortgagee. In essence this means you share in the proceeds of rental income given your existing position in the Devco. Your equity must remain with the Devco in order to maintain your entitlement to the proportionate share of rental income.

If the developer buys out your interest, then the Devco is entirely owned by the developer and you take back your equity with a negotiated buyout.

If you retain your partnership but pull your equity out, you would either have to negotiate a new partnership to share in the rental income or give that up altogether. Whatever this new position becomes, will drive if or how much you share in rental income. The bigger likelihood is, if you pull your equity out, that you would also have to subdivide the property. The house you own being one lot and the rental property as the second

LANDOWNER/ ALSO KI_3: This is sounding less attractive somehow and more complicated.

RESEARCHER: *Yes, and I need you to understand just that; but it can be made to work and there are other options. If this were a longer-term goal, say as legacy for your family while generating income in the interim—you could take back your title and buy out the developer after the profits are reconciled, with cash or separate financing.*

Then YOU would own everything and can do whatever you like. As an investment strategy, it would also be much easier to re-finance something that is built, occupied and already generating an income stream.

This can be a compelling option if you can afford to do it. I completed a rental triplex (three units, with three additional basement suites) on a single family lot with a colleague a few years ago. He converted his construction loan into a long-term mortgage. He was the owner/ developer and so he just had to hire a builder. That project of course was not BAAKFIL, but it was a terrific learning experience.

Another option of course is to simply take back title, buy one of the new units from the Devco and then rent it out. That is another rental scenario that is clean and simple.

Depending upon the number of units available—buying one to rent out could yield some interesting investment opportunities. With the pie lot demonstration project the additional number of units compared to your property can yield a profit share to the landowner to support buying one of the new units to rent with a smaller mortgage than what they had when they first bought.

LANDOWNER/ ALSO KI_3: OK. Is a co-op model an option too?

RESEARCHER: *This becomes even more complicated and it starts with the question of scale.*

A co-op usually has a critical mass of units to be feasible. However, some are simply small

buildings like townhouses while others can be hundreds of units in an apartment typology. CMHC outlines in its Co-op Housing Guide the general criteria that apply but co-op legislation varies across the country.

In Alberta a co-op is a non-profit self-governed organization and there are rules about its dissolution as to whom the remaining assets can be distributed. Technically, property must be transferred to another co-op, a non-profit organization or a charitable organization. If you are still part of the Devco and it is non-profit; then I would expect the terms of reference for the co-op as set up through legal counsel, to address dissolution, if it is your desire to have the property revert to you or to your estate at some point. I am not clear what this would entail but I suspect it could be done.

As a viable model for moderating housing cost to the consumer (no down payments, right to tenure etc.), there may come a time where co-op structuring could be modified. As you know this is effectively another form of renting—somewhere in between ownership and rent—unless it is an equity model.

Ontario co-op corporations for example, enable unit shares to be sold at market value for gain. This is different but not available everywhere. Most housing in New York City for example is a form of equity co-op too.

Back to your site, a co-op might make more sense than subdividing property unless you had a larger property with the possibility of many units and you are not part of the co-op. In any case this represents a longer-term strategy and it is likely not the best option based on your situation since, in effect, you would be contributing but suspending your equity interest without meaningful monetary gain. This goes to the bigger idea of housing as an asset class in a portfolio versus changing market conditions where housing is just a home for someone. This of course also goes to the bigger housing question. In the case of rental, the cash flow is shared according to the proportionate ownership of the development company, net after mortgage payments. It is much simpler.

In both cases title to the property remains with the Devco or the co-op as long as there is bank financing in place where the title is pledged against it; unless you can trigger one of the buyout options I described. It is flexible; but the co-op model might not work for you as much as it might for others across the country.

LANDOWNER/
ALSO KI_3:
I see the picture more clearly now but it is a lot to digest.

Yes, these ideas need gestation time and I am certainly not a real estate specialist or legal analyst. The rental or co-op model as a start-up scenario, is more complicated, whereas the condo model is straight forward.

For co-op and rental, the lender needs to see a cash flow proforma and be convinced the construction loan/long-term mortgage can be retired in a traditional fashion, so obviously there is more risk with this model.

Other financiers like pension funds, mortgage brokers or trust companies, may offer other incentives for longer-term deals (so-called 'patient capital') but I am again choosing to rely on the traditional banking sector for proof of concept. And I would always seek legal advice.

LANDOWNER/
ALSO KI_3:
We love living where we are and this gets even better with LRT expansion. I like the idea of BAAKFIL conceptually regardless of condo, rent or co-op because in our case, having our son and his young family closer to us would bring wonderful side benefits. The yard takes a lot of upkeep and as we get older, I am tired of having to deal with that and snow removal, for example. They'd pitch in to ease that burden. I think that the idea of bringing a family closer together if they want to be and doing this by simply giving up a bit of land can actually be a pretty good marketing strategy.

In our case, the property would stay in the family too and all of it would be theirs someday. If we did this, we'd find the simplest solution available from what you describe and it certainly seems there are a lot of possibilities.

But in the end and this is a big question—are you confident that people will pay up to half a million dollars for a small piece of property in a backyard?

At first glance this may sound unlikely to a pragmatic thinker and I have heard this from others as well. It is a fair question. I have struggled with that idea myself, but I think you have answered it already too. Your own situation brings the benefit of knowing who you would be selling or renting to and that is your family. I would think that is a huge factor.

To others, the idea of building a micro-community or a naturally occurring retirement community (NORC) on a site–such as my pie lot demonstration project, has merit as well.

I certainly conclude BAAKFIL is not for everyone, which is another reason for only using a conservative 25% support for the idea over 25 years. Second, the costs are all relative and we aren't talking about $500,000 as the start point in any case, but again, I understand the question. It still seems like a lot of money and it is, but to keep it in perspective, the average cost of a single family house in Edmonton is still around $500,000 and across Canada closer to $800,000. Home ownership is a fleeting possibility for many. The 2022 Canada census predicts a larger percentage of the population in the next 25 years will be renters, given the increasing cost of entering the ownership market.

This discussion took us into a lot of detail, so I will close by summarizing why I believe in the potential of the business model to improve an ownership circumstance such as yours by monetizing your asset as you age in place.

BAAKFIL is a flexible model despite rising costs because everything is relative. Land will always continue to escalate in value. BAAKFIL can consistently address land attainability and increase (relative) affordability by removing this land cost from the housing supply challenge—no matter where the market lands. Bankers I speak with say the model itself is not really impacted by inflation because again, all the costs are relative. If the market says it is worth it, if the banks say you can borrow enough to pay for it and then pay them back over time; the numbers don't matter to them. This is a basic economics argument and a stark reality of the banking industry. They love debt, so long as they remain whole.

Unfortunately it seems clear that the base line cost definition of affordability will need to keep increasing to new levels, given the reality of this wicked problem. As such BAAKFIL is no panacea, but as in your case, you can be on the receiving end of a financial spike with a sale or a steady additional income stream if renting without putting up any cash as you grow older and bring your family closer together, building their future on the same property.

Consumer KI*_11

RESEARCHER: *This journey with the two of you began in 2019 to search for property for a custom infill project. As two working professionals, an engineer and owner of a beauty salon, you wanted to work on-line from home even before Covid and install the salon on the property too. You also had an original idea about what you call a 'near suite', a self-contained unit for both sets of parents to share so they can each live with you at different times during the year. Such a wonderful idea and a different take on intergenerational living. The city bylaws allow for huge infill but still restrict land use so, regardless of garden suites and laneway housing, you did not fit into any box back then and we had to figure out how this could be done.*

You spent a year earlier going to open houses, talking with the City and, after finding nothing suitable, you reached out to me to help navigate the minefields of site selection, program, budget and to design your forever home.

This coincided with my starting into the DDes program and at the time BAAKFIL was nowhere to be imagined.

So let's summarize where you have been and where you see this going next.

CONSUMER KI*_11: You just did! We were attracted to your INFILLHAUS project initially and hoped we could do something like that to respect the neighbourhood we would find and satisfy our needs as well. We saw dozens of properties and infill lots before you and with you; some with old houses and some just vacant land and they ranged from $360,000 to $600,000. This is way more than we expected when we started with a total budget of $750,000. The City had one property that you saw and they put it up for auction with a stipulated price minimum offer of $567,000. We are still looking, thinking that interest rate increases and a softening market will bring better opportunities. Canadian Emergency Response Benefit (CERB) won't last forever, mortgage deferrals are ending, there was a slowdown of people moving into the city last year and so on; but as you suggest, this is just not working for us. Maybe we need a Plan B.

Edmonton is still seen as one of the best real estate markets for housing prices in Canada but where we have been is frustrating.

We love the prototype infill concept you did for us, similar to INFILLHAUS that can adapt to an east–west or north–south lot, but we just can't get the numbers to work with land at $400,000. Zoning was a big challenge too, but that seems to be changing with the new draft Bylaws.

RESEARCHER: *Yes we figured out how we could do the salon attached to the house. The initial idea you had was to build a garage with a garden suite above it, but that was expensive. Garden suites now are more than $350,000 today since most people end up building a new garage first with proper foundations, so they make them as large as they can. City servicing and connection charges add up and so on. It is not economical in the long run. Laneway housing in Toronto too is well over $1,000,000 right now. These typologies produce some innovative one–off projects, but they aren't scalable.*

I know you have had to increase your budget as a result of land attainability and cost challenges. Covid hasn't helped either schedule-wise. You are looking at more than 2800sf of program and a budget more than $1,000,000 if the land is factored in at around $400,000. That is the average land cost of all the properties you've seen. Since they were all in mature neighbourhoods though— which is my research area—I have been thinking of testing BAAKFIL as an option with you, now that it has become more than a concept.

CONSUMER KI*_11: The BAAKFIL proposal that you showed us is interesting, but we are pretty sure this is not what we are looking for.

You reviewed the proposal we got from the builder who is marketing new infill and we thought that it could be made to work for our needs, but it was a house designed for $568,000 excluding land, the near suite would be in the basement and we'd still have to extend the house to fit in my small salon, so we are right back at the million dollar number and likely more, depending on the land cost.

And it looks like from how you explained building orientation to us, that his plans would work best on a north–south lot, limiting our property choices even more.

RESEARCHER: *That was a good exercise to go through, but the plan is being sold as a product. This is the house building industry manifesting itself in mature neighbourhoods. Any changes and it is going to cost more. How would they address your first concern of not having the near suite in a basement? I don't think they could with that design; so you would be spending money and compromising something really important to you.*

Shall we play a what–if scenario?

CONSUMER KI*_11: BAAKFIL?

RESEARCHER: *I have shown you my pie lot demonstration project. Maybe we should try and shift 'the ask' a little to start. You can find some solid post-war mature neighbourhood houses in most of the areas where you are looking. The King Edward property had me thinking that the existing house could be easily expanded since it is on a corner lot. The site faces a park and was on the market for $359,000 in 2021 when we saw it. It was empty so it didn't show well and stayed on the market for a while. Instead of spending $50,000 to tear it down today, then build my infill prototype, that money could replace fixtures, carpets and upgrade either the bathroom or the kitchen. That house could be cleaned up if available today and rented out while you stay in your townhouse. During that time, we could design a BAAKFIL unit that faces both the back alley and the avenue. This could be your living space with the salon at a lower level and parking included for your one at a time customers, off the alley.*

CONSUMER KI*_11: How does renting the house help us achieve what we want?

It doesn't, other than provide you some cash flow for a year to reduce your overall time costs of doing the development. The key though is to remove the land cost from your situation too, which is the key to BAAKFIL and the affordability piece.

It is a small house with a finished basement. The main level might be a great fit as your 'near suite'. In fact, with two bedrooms, it could probably be set up as a joint 'near suite' so from time to time both your parents could be there. At least they could overlap their stays over the holidays or special occasions.

The finished basement could be your storage, workshop and weight room; perhaps even the laundry, so you aren't spending money building storage and utility space at today's prices.

The big idea would be to connect the existing house to the new BAAKFIL unit with a shared sitting or eating space that overlooks a sunny little courtyard between the two houses. It could be a similar layout to the generic one I did for you that tested the infill prototype.

In this case, you would be the 'first' and 'second' consumer and I'd be testing the versatility of BAAKFIL.

First, you buy a property and fix up the existing house for the same price or thereabouts as you would be paying for a subdivided bare land infill lot. Generate some cash flow by renting for the year we build. Then commit BAAKFIL!

Then you become the developer and the owner and you take the land cost out of the new construction equation because it is already built into the existing house.

CONSUMER KI*_11: Well you have certainly talked a lot about the things that people hate about how infill is currently going. So many infills start with tearing houses down. So much just goes to the landfill. Thinking about it, that is certainly not how we want to start building good relations in a neighbourhood. OK, tell us how much this idea is going to cost us moving forward.

I knew that was coming. I don't know. We don't have a site or a house to examine yet but let's stick with King Edward for now to build out the argument. It was on the market for $359,000 so for argument's sake say we find something like that today for $400,000. A 1000sf house including finished basement on a 40x140 lot. Put $50,000 into a renovation fund. If you are finding sturdy housing in Edmonton, there is usually fir framing, cementitious stucco and hardwood flooring. Good bones.

Next we take the land out of the equation so for $200–225/sf we build the remainder of your program which is 1600sf that is interestingly the biggest BAAKFIL layout with a 24x24 footprint over three levels. There is no basement, so the salon can be on the lower level and you'd live in the upper two, and we'd add another space to connect the two units. Maybe it is 200sf or so (8x24).

So you are adding 1800sf of new space at $225/sf or say $405,000. Using rough numbers

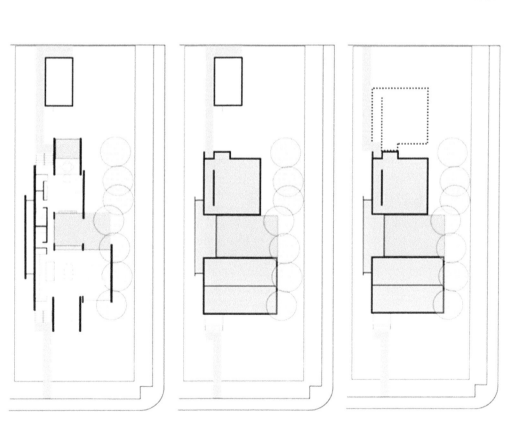

▲ Figure 4.2.3

New Infill prototype, BAAKFIL/existing house/BAAKFIL expanded

this adds up to $855,000. Once we build a few BAAKFIL projects we will have a better idea of the costs but this is definitely at the upper end. This is better than your revised budget because you aren't buying just land for $400,000. I am doing one other demonstration project on a corner lot in addition to my pie lot and the developer is using $175/sf for new construction but the building finishes are mid-range and not what you have requested, but I know $225/sf is solid right now for you in Edmonton.

Since you are the developer, the value of the property in its improved state is worth up to 15–25% more than when you start if we were to 'invert' the model and think of it as a project, living in one unit and selling the other.

CONSUMER KI*_11: I never thought of this before. This is going to cause a few long nights thinking it through, but it sure could change the way we can continue looking at property.

We know there are still many cute little ones around that are nice for considerably less than the average cost of $500,000 and certainly the King Edward house fits that profile. On the surface, I like the logic and the idea of a sunny courtyard separating the two units would be great.

RESEARCHER: *Maybe we should end it here. But I want to tell you one more thing first that comes to mind. It is not directly applicable to you, at least not yet, because your folks are still relatively young.*

But I am reminded of a conversation I had with a colleague recently about BAAKFIL and its intergenerational living potential and how changing demographics with smaller households are impacting the marketplace.

You are both working professionals with no children, you have your own company and so you fit that changing cohort. The point I am coming to is my colleague observed that in evaluating BAAKFIL we might think about it 25 years from now and examine that context too.

BAAKFIL is intended to adapt to changing times right now and my chosen window is a 25-year (one generation) transition. What he is asking is how sustainable is BAAKFIL to adapt to changing times for another 25 years? What might that mean?

We expect our housing stock in Alberta to last for at least three generations (seventy-five years) or more. Our old house was built in the 1950s and it just sold again for a lot more than what we got for it 20 years ago. So, while this is not the research question I am addressing— longevity adaptability—it is a very compelling and realistic question.

What will housing look like in Alberta or in all of Canada in 25 years? Does BAAKFIL morph into something else? Can it? Separate living and common amenities for everyone like say a co-habitation model? With increased immigration, and families beginning to consolidate smaller households together already, will we look to and import other forms of intergenerational living from other cultures over time? Will shared living, dining, shared food preparation, sleeping, play— like separate pavilions—provide independence for a living family 'tree'? Is that how we might get around the dearth of seniors' care facilities in the future? Does BAAKFIL have a role to play?

I am outside the scope of my research here; but I can't help ponder this, given your own lifestyle aspirations. Inside the research though, your file is a great test of the business model and its adaptability. Maybe BAAKFIL fits into your future yet, we'll see.

Chapter 5

BAAKFIL Design Tool-Kit

5.1 Introduction

BAAKFIL demonstrates the principles of the business model, gentle densification, demographics and affordability in a separately published booklet. It is included in this chapter.

The Tool-kit advocates that projects respect the context of mature residential neighbourhoods. This separates BAAKFIL from the product-oriented repetition of the house building industry.

A flexible typology (*innovation of things*), BAAKFIL is scalable for standalone, multi-unit or cottage court group configurations.

Plans are based on an unassuming building footprint no larger than a standard double car garage. This familiar size and scale is an important step to building community support for the concept in mature neighbourhoods.

A general 24′ x 24′ (7200mm x 7200mm) footprint is configured in foursquare 12′ x 12′ (3600mm x 3600mm) modules. It is a flexible pinwheel plan for up to three levels and no basement. The Tool-kit describes how this is achieved, including sample designs to illustrate a systems approach to economical sustainable building design, including a net zero target.

Regional characteristics, local building systems, advanced technology and material choices respond to economics, site and demographic specificity. This enables architects, designers and house builders to consider BAAKFIL as a planning strategy in their own communities across the country.

The basic principles include:

- BAAKFIL starts with standard wood frame construction and basic industry skill sets.
- It takes the housing industry into a predominantly ignored design realm where site orientation, access to sunlight, wind protection, privacy, scale and topography are given due consideration.
- A sustainable design strategy—an infrastructure core—is an efficient, adaptable backbone that enables technological advances such as the inclusion of photovoltaics, geothermal and earth tube AC systems.

The foursquare module allows efficient room sizes, side by side with plan configurations that can be modified and 'torqued' around a central axis to adapt to climate and site orientation.

This enables a suite of unit options and interchangeable layouts with defined circulation, small but gracious living spaces and myriad configurations. This ordering strategy and a basic level of construction detailing is not a prescription for repetition. It is rather an idea-primer for a respectful and bespoke densification typology that is constructible *within* the house building industry.

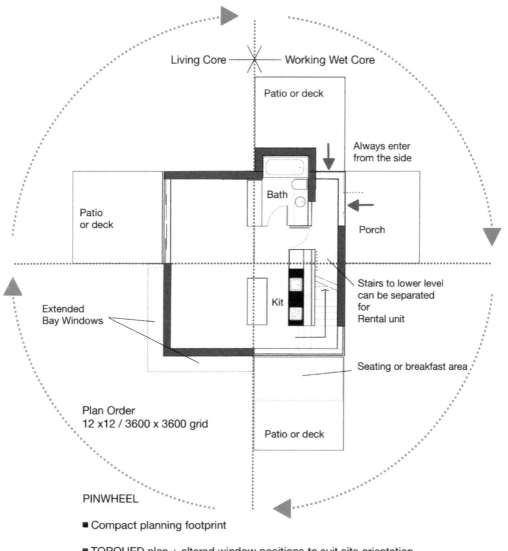

Living Core — Working Wet Core

Patio or deck

Always enter
from the side

Bath

Patio
or deck

Porch

Extended
Bay Windows

Kit

Stairs to lower level
can be separated
for
Rental unit

Seating or breakfast area

Plan Order
12 x12 / 3600 x 3600 grid

Patio or deck

PINWHEEL

■ Compact planning footprint

■ TORQUED plan + altered window positions to suit site orientation

▲ Figure 5.1.1

The Pinwheel Plan

By inspiring architects, designers and builders to use the Tool-kit to take their own projects to another level in their region, this means that no two units need to be the same, again separating BAAKFIL from design homogeneity.

The Tool-kit can also be used independently of the business model.

Two demonstration projects are inspired by the Tool-kit design principles and are featured in Chapter 6.

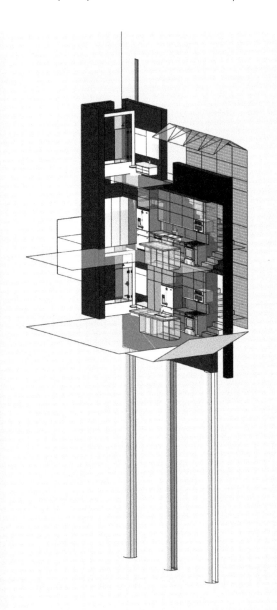

◀ Figure 5.1.2

Infrastructure Core

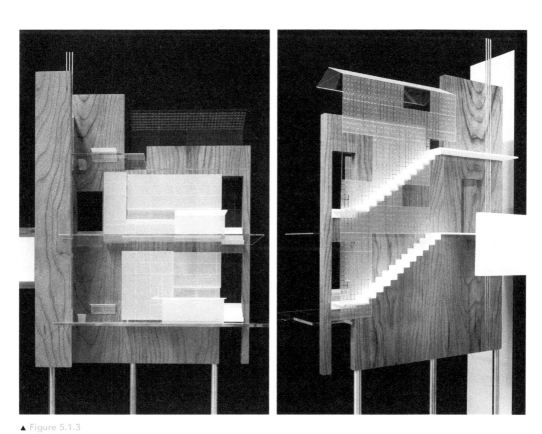

▲ Figure 5.1.3

Abstract Model Infrastructure Core (model by Ellis Associates)

The following pages illustrate the BAAKFIL Tool-kit booklet in its entirety.

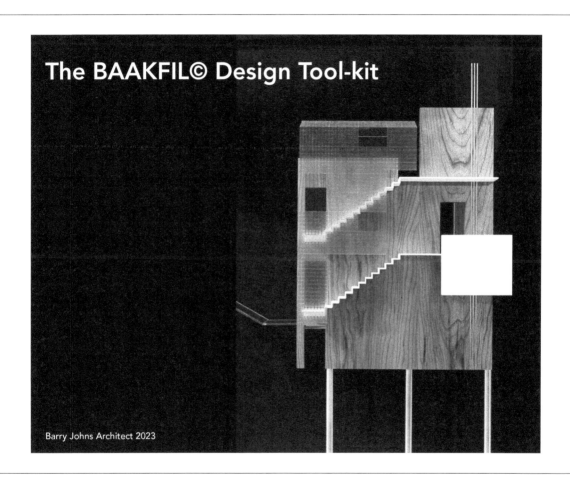

The BAAKFIL© Design Tool-kit

Barry Johns Architect 2023

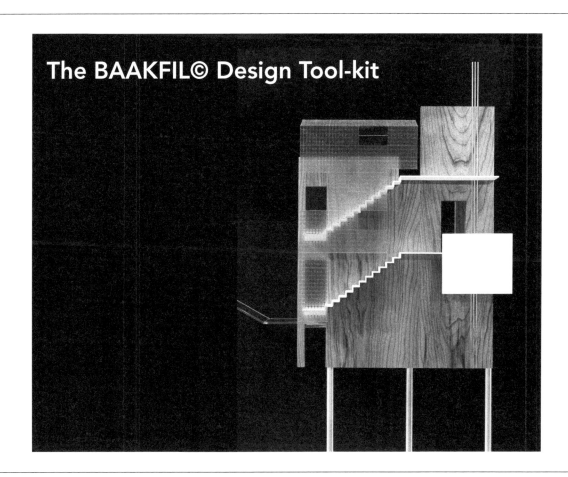

The BAAKFIL© Design Tool-kit

Chapter 5 BAAKFIL Design Tool-Kit

Contents

5.2 The BAAKFIL© Design Tool-kit

This publication is the **Design Tool-kit** component of a doctoral thesis by an Edmonton based architect. The dissertation addresses the housing crisis in Canada through an affordable and scalable densification agenda for urban neighbourhoods, with its focus in Edmonton, Alberta.

The thesis comprises a new business model *(innovation of ways)* for a missing middle typology called **BAAKFIL** *(innovation of things)*, as an alternative to *infill*—that promotes respectful densification by first retaining existing serviceable housing stock.

The business model brings a landowner into an investment partnership with a developer to jointly develop underused back yard space of a single family property to build something new; monetizing one's asset without putting up any cash, without needing to move and without changing the character of a neighbourhood streetscape. Land cost is removed from the developer proforma and new housing is instantly more affordable.

The **Design Tool-kit** offers a guideline to missing middle typologies, with examples that describe an ordered strategy as an idea-primer. Units are flexible yet provide defined circulation, stacked services, gracious living spaces and myriad configurations within a sustainable design framework. Architects, designers and builders can use this **Design Tool-kit** to influence the design of a project to bespoke levels in their own region. No two units need be the same—separating **BAAKFIL** from the commodified house building industry. The Tool-kit advances the principles of retention and gentle densification. It can also be used independently of the business model.

A video summary of *BAAKFIL* and the Design TOOL-KIT can be viewed at www. bjalstudio.ca

BAAKFIL isometric drawing
of infrastructure core showing
optional, stacked kitchen(s),
washroom(s), stair and envelope
configurations

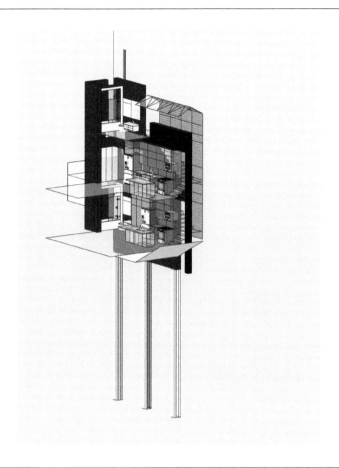

Background

Infill reduces sprawl by increasing density on single family urban lots. Its speculative deployment is however predicated on the demolition of serviceable housing stock with lots sold *at much higher land prices*; replaced by two skinny houses, often larger than the original house. With costs now beyond the $1M price point in many Canadian cities—this unintended consequence *contributes* to the housing affordability crisis *plus* the erosion of mature neighbourhoods. Restrictive, outdated zoning bylaws negate responsive planning and design while ignoring the needs of a changing demographic to an older population and smaller households. Respect for neighbourhoods is lost by demolition and over scaled product; impacting the character of existing streetscapes

BAAKFIL incorporates the smaller household into an underused rear yard; retaining the existing house, leaving the streetscape unchanged. With removal of land cost, affordability is increased. Thousands of lots across the country can accommodate this approach; yielding a scalable model for gentle densification in mature Canadian neighbourhoods.

BAAKFIL addresses 'city building' by increasing density and re-inventing the back alley—with sidewalks and commercial activity promoting neighbourhood interaction and safety. Gently developed over 25 years alongside updated flexible *zoning*, this transformation engages key ideas about the resilient, 15 minute walkable city.

BAAKFIL is an acronym for Back Alley Advantage, Kinship, Family & Integrated Living

Typical verdant mature neighbourhood block, illustrating retention of existing housing, preserved streetscapes and the nominal impact of a 25% density increase with new units no larger than a two car garage on existing lots and on surplus municipal land flanking major boulevard (left)

BAAKFIL incentivizes aging in community, alley revitalization and neighbourhood interaction while leaving neighbourhood streetscapes unchanged.

Background

The BAAKFIL Tool-kit is a set of design principles:

An urban design strategy that backfills downsized residential options into underused backyards, creating a micro-community and multigenerational or intergenerational living opportunities.

A set of spatial principles with a unique infrastructure core; the Tool-kit planning strategy is illustrated by examples that are ordered, flexible and scalable; adaptable to various socio-economic and site conditions.

The Tool-kit is not prescriptive. It is a generalization of possibilities—a catalyst for responsible site planning and multi-use design.

Architects, designers and builders can use the Tool-kit to inform their own work to meet the specific conditions of their communities across Canada.

Sample cottage court with existing
house and three new units, central
linear trellis courtyard, roof decks,
gardens and parking

This

Not This

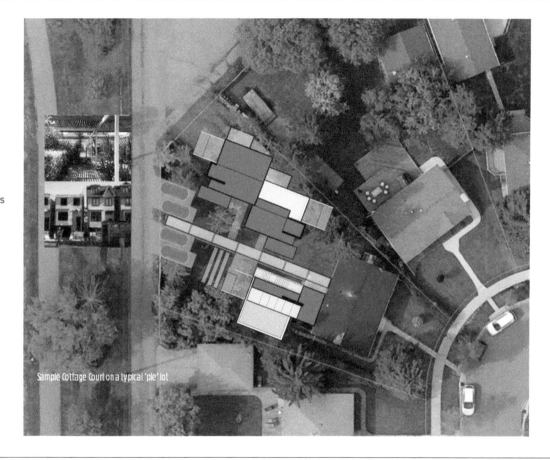

Sample Cottage Court on a typical 'pie' lot

The Pinwheel Plan

The Design Tool-kit is simple, predicated on building with conventional construction.

It is nevertheless poised to adapt broader technological advances—net zero, regeneration, mass customization and prefabrication, mass timber, 3d printing, digital twin intelligent building software—as the industry catches up.

BAAKFIL flexibility begins with a compact 24' x 24' (7200mm x 7200mm) footprint—a foursquare 12 foot (3600mm) module that yields efficient room sizes, side by side on standard 30' – 50' lot widths.

Based on a pinwheel, plans can be modified or 'torqued' around the centre axis—to be oriented specifically to climate and site.

The footprint is a consistently ordered plan, but porches, doors, windows and deck locations can be positioned almost anywhere to prioritize rooms or spaces with access to views, wind protection or to capture the sun; depending upon site and program requirements.

Site planning principles of pinwheel
plan with sun, wind and view
orientation taken into consideration

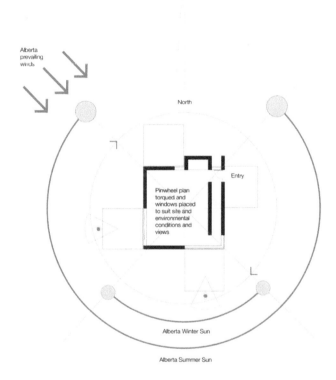

The Pinwheel Plan

The planning module accommodates room expansion or contraction with different roof, window and wall configurations and materials. Porches, decks, patios, bay and extended window assemblies are all possible within this compact footprint.

BAAKFIL can align with personal taste or the character of a neighbourhood.

A bespoke residence can be derived from simple principles, ensuring that *BAAKFIL* negates the predictable homogeneity of mass housing developments.

The 24 x 24 base planning module also adapts to derivative modules of:

20 x 20 (6000mm x 6000mm)
22 x 22 (6600mm x 6600mm)
22 x 24 (6600mm x 7200mm)

These are equivalent to the footprint of standard double car garages that exist everywhere, often purchased as kits from home building suppliers. This building form is so common to neighbourhoods across the country that community groups can quickly understand the unthreatening scale of a BAAKFIL proposal.

Pinwheel planning principles -
consistent location of infrastructure
core elements and appropriate,
flexible site orientation

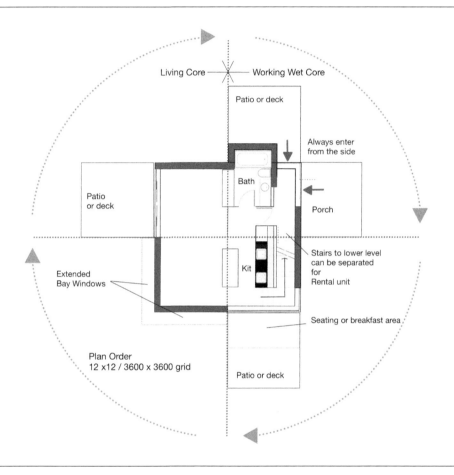

Living Core ——✕—— Working Wet Core

Patio or deck

Always enter
from the side

Bath

Patio
or deck

Porch

Stairs to lower level
can be separated
for
Rental unit

Kit

Extended
Bay Windows

Seating or breakfast area

Plan Order
12 x12 / 3600 x 3600 grid

Patio or deck

The Pinwheel Plan

Layouts with the infrastructure core can be simply *torqued* to respond to site and climate orientation.

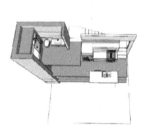 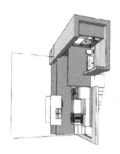 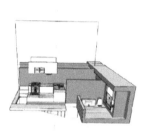 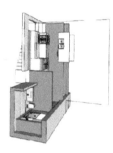

Alternate, flexible floor plans over
three levels

Plan Order

Lower Suite

Studio

Bedrooms

Main

Upper Loft

open

The Infrastructure Core

The backbone of BAAKFIL, the infrastructure core is an integrated planning and service strategy influenced by Louis Kahn's original definition of servant and served space.

The *Servant* space is a consolidated collection of:

- Stairs
- Kitchens (with variable sizes and layout) appliances and millwork
- Baths
- Storage
- Energy infrastructure
- Components can be prefabricated or customized
- Services can be stacked

The *Served* spaces—living, working, eating, sleeping can be open or enclosed with a module space width of 12′.

The core elements—typically de-centralised in a builder residence—are concentrated, leading to economies of scale and services distribution. As a *parti*, the core enables flexible room layouts, exposure, design expression and cost effective construction, adaptable to changing technologies.

View of abstract infrastructure core
kitchen and bathroom modules

View of infrastructure core stair and
abstract exterior skin options

The Infrastructure Core

Services are stacked. Wet vertical services are placed on the inside wall, with horizontal services feeding from it through a floor or ceiling plenum.

BAAKFIL is net zero ready—the core can accommodate nature-based or technical innovations:

- Stacked plumbing, electrical and mechanical distribution reduces material quantities, bends and site coordination challenges, yielding economical construction with base materials.
- The natural insulating characteristics of the earth work at no cost, with the building perimeter let into the ground to reduce the exposure of the envelope to the elements.
- Earth tube cooling is a natural system derived from installing continuous lengths of plastic pipe below the frost line to enable outdoor air to be drawn through it into a structure via an in-line fan. The natural insulating characteristics of the earth mean that ambient temperatures averaging 55 degrees F naturally cool fresh air to eliminate the need for air conditioning.
- The use of solar panels as an add-on after market product, is being superseded by efficient and increasingly cost effective innovations, such as photovoltaic assemblies where energy can be harvested within skin and roof materials integrated with the building envelope.

Net zero infrastructure core design
principles as described

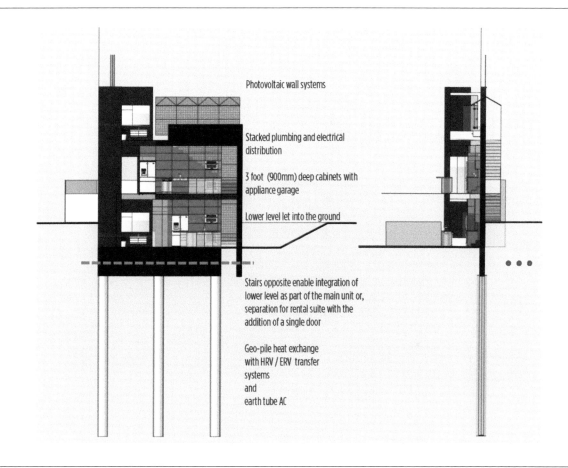

Photovoltaic wall systems

Stacked plumbing and electrical
distribution

3 foot (900mm) deep cabinets with
appliance garage

Lower level let into the ground

Stairs opposite enable integration of
lower level as part of the main unit or,
separation for rental suite with the
addition of a single door

Geo-pile heat exchange
with HRV / ERV transfer
systems
and
earth tube AC

The Infrastructure Core

- Heat pumps can be used with geo-pile foundations that are natural energy capture systems that use carrier fluid piping installed inside the reinforcing cage of a structural pile foundation. Heat can be extracted from or injected into the ground with earth assist to absorb heating and cooling loads. This can also include pre-heating domestic hot water prior to being distributed to a tank-less hot water system.
- The 12″ (300mm) thickness of the core wall accommodates small, higher velocity ductwork in HRV/ERV heat recovery systems, reducing the extent of branch ductwork that often interferes with other services. Loft areas can in effect be ductless, with direct discharge or extraction .
- The core wall thickness enables standard two foot (600mm) counter depths to be increased to 3 feet (900mm) to provide deep pull out lower storage bins and appliance storage at the counter level. Increasing storage in compact spaces, appliance 'garages' are standard details in the practice and are used for kitchenware, glassware and appliances.
- Integration of doors with millwork eliminates cumbersome rough carpentry framing for closets and service rooms. Prefabricated panels or doors reduce cost and increase net usable area.

Net zero infrastructure core interior
design principles as described

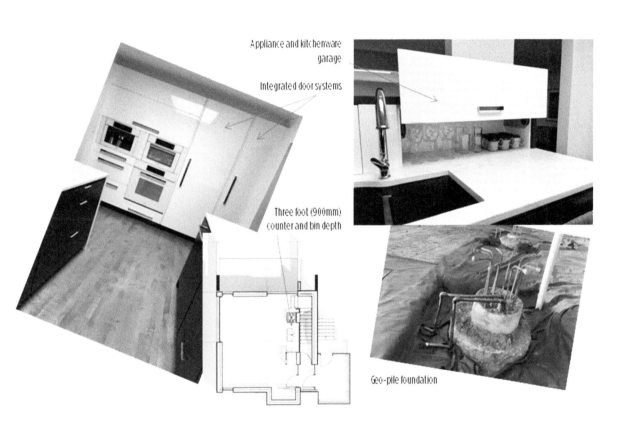

Appliance and kitchenware
garage

Integrated door systems

Three foot (900mm)
counter and bin depth

Geo-pile foundation

BAAKFIL Construction Adaptability

Material selection and design detailing is not limited with BAAKFIL.

Within a 12" (300mm) thick envelope (or more) higher R values with traditional or new products and finishes, can result in a net zero strategy using floor, wall and roof configurations best suited to the location where BAAKFIL is situated.

Within this flexible matrix, architects, designers and builders can adapt their work to enable innovations from 3D printing, prefabrication, mass customization, proprietary building products, digital-twin intelligent building software, all pointing to net zero carbon buildings, when and where the market supports these initiatives.

BAAKFIL supports the NECB, BC Step Codes, Green Energy Futures, and other sustainable building performance metrics.

Construction wall section at typical
main level between lower floor and
main floor

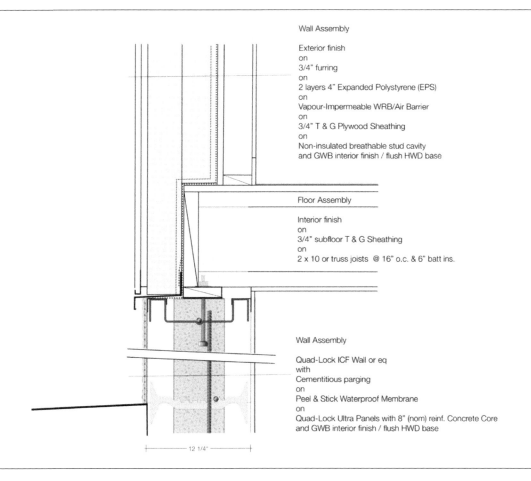

Wall Assembly

Exterior finish
on
3/4" furring
on
2 layers 4" Expanded Polystyrene (EPS)
on
Vapour-Impermeable WRB/Air Barrier
on
3/4" T & G Plywood Sheathing
on
Non-insulated breathable stud cavity
and GWB interior finish / flush HWD base

Floor Assembly

Interior finish
on
3/4" subfloor T & G Sheathing
on
2 x 10 or truss joists @ 16" o.c. & 6" batt ins.

Wall Assembly

Quad-Lock ICF Wall or eq
with
Cementitious parging
on
Peel & Stick Waterproof Membrane
on
Quad-Lock Ultra Panels with 8" (nom) reinf. Concrete Core
and GWB interior finish / flush HWD base

12 1/4"

BAAKFIL Site Planning Adaptability

To enable flexibility and accommodate various sized lots, BAAKFIL units can be combined to create duplex and/or missing middle 'cottage court' typologies to increase density on larger properties such as corner, 'pie' or irregularly sized lots.

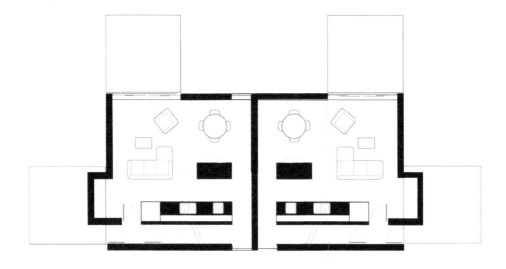

▲ Figure 5.1.16

Two units combined in line with infrastructure core aligned

Two units combined, offset with
infrastructure core opposite

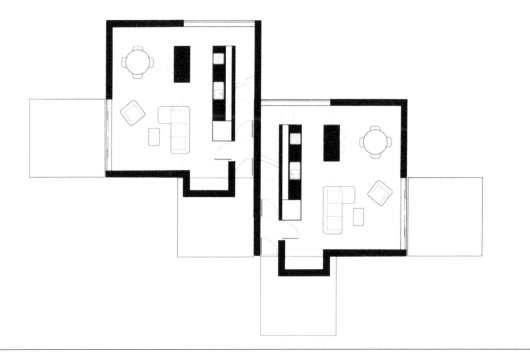

BAAKFIL Typology Adaptability

BAAKFIL accommodates flexible kitchen sizes, loft space, roof decks, roof porches and future expansion.

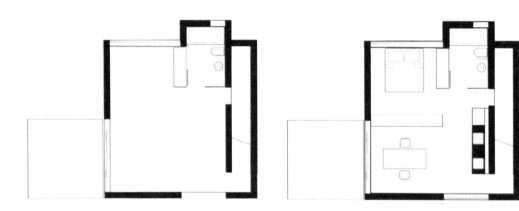

▲ Figure 5.1.18

Basic plan of infrastructure core
and open living loft space

▲ Figure 5.1.19

Basic plan of infrastructure core
and bedroom / work space

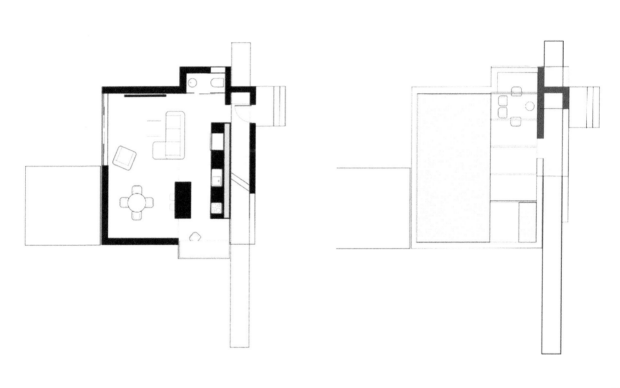

▲ Figure 5.1.20

Basic plan of infrastructure core, kitchen and living space

▲ Figure 5.1.21

Basic plan of infrastructure core and upper deck, trellis, garden

BAAKFIL Typology Adaptability

BAAKFIL accommodates amenity spaces and unit configurations over one, two or three levels.

With no basement, the lower level can be let into the ground where soils conditions allow and reduce scale while providing intimate, private patio and living spaces.

Co-joined Units

▲ Figure 5.1.22

Co-joined in line symmetrical units

Small single BAAKFIL unit with roof
deck and green roof

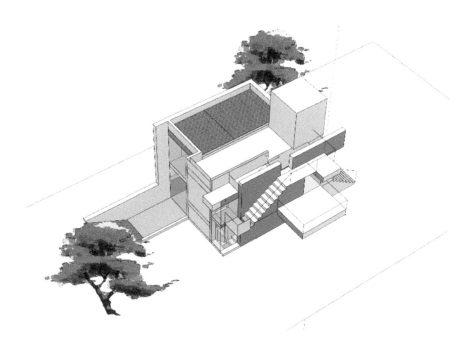

External or internal stairs and roof amenities

BAAKFIL Typology Adaptability

BAAKFIL accommodates amenity spaces and unit configurations over one, two or three levels.

    With no basement, the lower level can be let into the ground where soils conditions allow and reduce scale while providing intimate, private patio and living spaces.

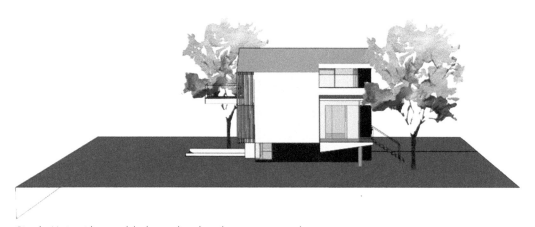

Single Unit with rentable lower level and common porch

▲ Figure 5.1.24

Unit with lower rental suite and porch entrance

Unit with interior vertical hydroponics
and green roof

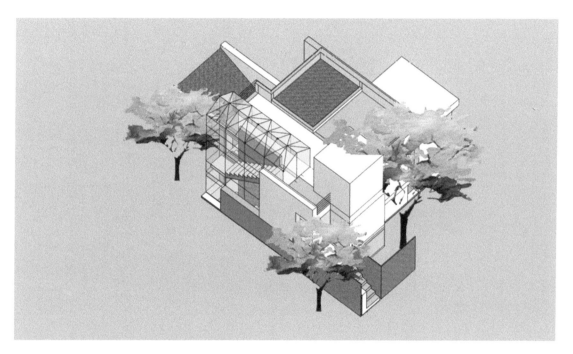

Urban agriculture interior and exterior

BAAKFIL Typology Adaptability

BAAKFIL accommodates roof deck amenities convertible to trellis patios, porches and internal expansion. This can be accommodated with single or two level units.

▲ Figure 5.1.26

Perspective view with green roof, deck and trellis

Roof plan with green roof, deck and trellis

BAAKFIL Typology Adaptability

BAAKFIL is net zero ready as it can accommodate numerous technologies such as photovoltaics, geo-piles, earth tube AC and HRV / ERV systems.

Net zero BAAKFIL unit with
photovoltaic wall and roof panels

BAAKFIL Typology Adaptability _ Universality

The 2021 Canadian Census validates the predictions of the 2016 Census. Canada is now officially an aged population. The baby boomer generation is rapidly becoming older, retiring, downsizing and increasingly infirmed.

- 19% of the population is 65 or older
- 22% of the population is between 55 and 64.

Universal design and living for seniors to thrive, by aging in community without being institutionalized is forecast to be a growth industry in the housing market.

BAAKFIL can become a leader in this area.

Layouts can be designed to incorporate future universal access with ramps, lifts and accessories. Unit designs can enable independent living, hobbies, co-dependent living, live-in health care or part-time health care, all within a multigenerational or intergenerational context next to family.

Universal floor plan showing
alternate lift

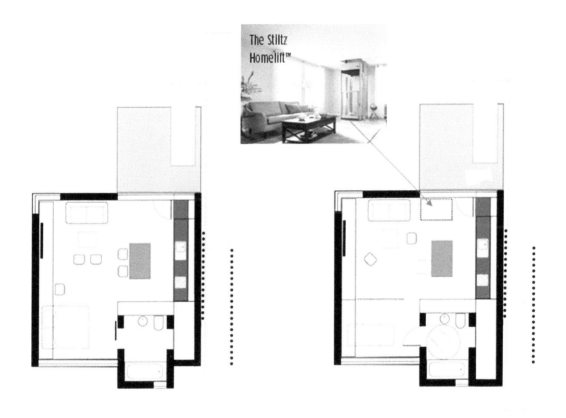

BAAKFIL Typology Adaptability _ Universality

The generic BAAKFIL universal unit can be a self contained single storey (per previous page) with an external stair and roof deck for able bodied and independent persons.

The roof deck can be developed into a second floor bedroom or studio for the occupant or his or her health care resident in the future with an internal lift connecting both levels. The lift can home base at the second level leaving the floor area of the main living floor unimpeded.

Perspective universal unit with roof deck and sloped entry terrace

Alternate universal plan with external
stair, lift and upper bedroom

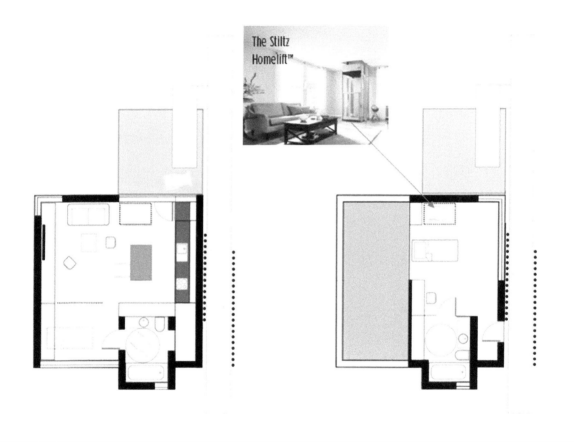

BAAKFIL Typology Adaptability _ Cottage Court / Corner lots

BAAKFIL accommodates corner lots in addition to internal and pie lots.

Larger developments are also possible with neighbours partnering together.

Single BAAKFIL unit and existing residence

▼ Figure 5.1.33

Double BAAKFIL unit and existing
residence

▼ Figure 5.1.34

Four BAAKFIL courtyard units on two
sites with two existing residences

BAAKFIL Typology Adaptability _
Hillside Studio

BAAKFIL accommodates sloped sites.

▲ Figure 5.1.35

Existing house site plan with view
on sloped site

▲ Figure 5.1.36

Studio plan buried into hillside

▼ Figure 5.1.37

Green roof and deck plan at patio
level of house

▼ Figure 5.1.38

Elevation of studio at house showing
sloped site

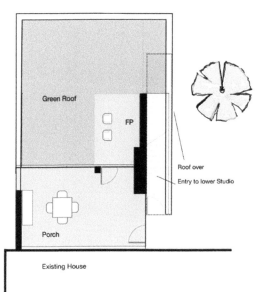

BAAKFIL Typology Adaptability _ House Renovations

BAAKFIL accommodates additions and renovations to existing residential units.

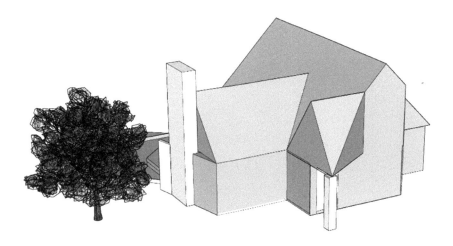

▲ Figure 5.1.39

Isometric of existing country residence

Isometric of BAAKFIL addition
(left side)

Elevation BAAKFIL
addition (left side)

BAAKFIL Typology Adaptability _ Smaller Footprint

BAAKFIL accommodates a smaller footprint such as 20 x 20 (6000mm x 6000mm) or 22 x 22 (6600mm x 6600mm) on a single level.

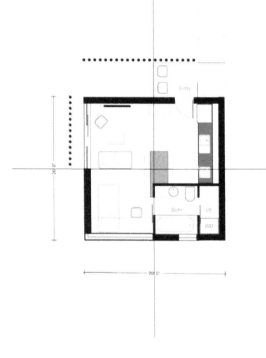

▲ Figure 5.1.42

Suspended double bed in floor position

▲ Figure 5.1.43

Suspended double bed in concealed ceiling position

▲ Figure 5.1.44

Small unit 20 x20 plan – twin bed shown dotted

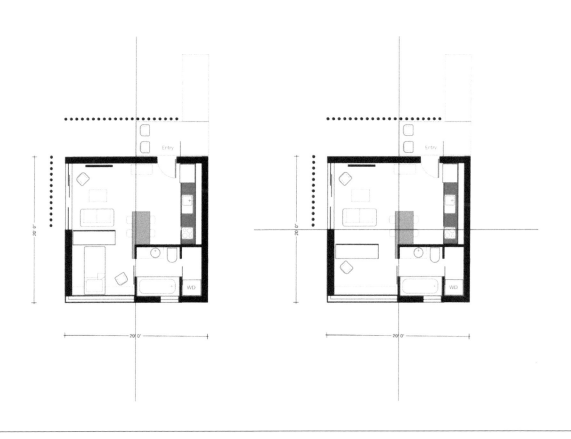

▲ Figure 5.1.45

Small unit 20 x 20 plan – twin Murphy
bed in place

▲ Figure 5.1.46

Small unit 20 x 20 plan -
twin Murphy bed upright / closed

BAAKFIL Typology Adaptability _ The 2 Car Garage

BAAKFIL accommodates *existing* 2 car garages, when foundations and building shell can be retained or upgraded.

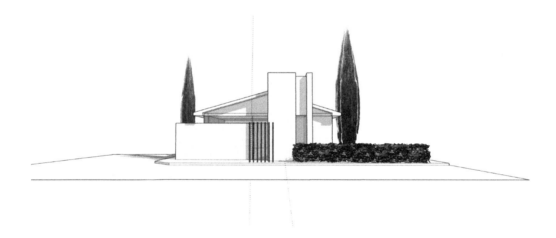

▲ Figure 5.1.47

24 x 22 double garage modified to BAAKFIL

24 x 22 double garage modified -
BAAKFIL plan

BAAKFIL©

Barry Johns Architect 2023
780 499 8989
bjstudio@shaw.ca
www.bjalstudio.ca

Isometric infrastructure core concept
with sloped roof

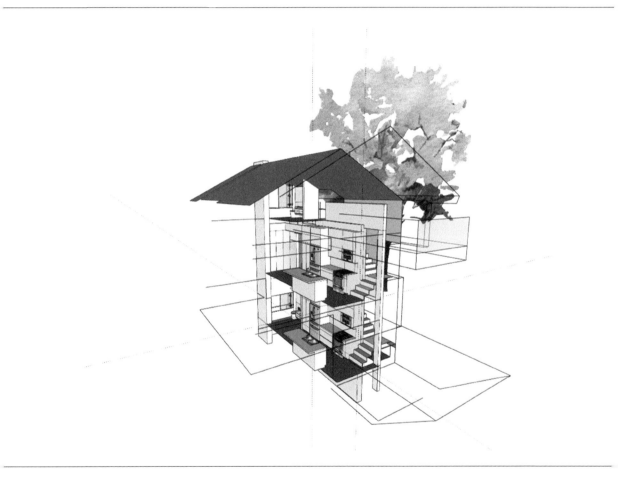

6.1 Demonstration Projects 1 + 2

BAAKFIL is presented in two projects, using the business model and the Design Tool-kit to interrogate the gentle densification idea and graphically illustrate design possibilities.

Demonstration Project No. 1

This is the primary project of this dissertation and embodies the scope of BAAKFIL typologies. It imagines the development of three BAAKFIL units on a site in Dovercourt, Edmonton. This is a neighbourhood largely built up by the early 1960s. The area is walkable and well served by transit. It is close to the oldest shopping mall in the city and has reasonable access to downtown, the west end office industrial area, schools and recreation centres.

The site is a typical pie lot of approximately 10,000sf (930sm) and the existing house is a small three-bedroom bungalow (1040sf/96sm) plus finished basement. The main floor is situated three feet (900mm) above grade, enabling windows in the basement. To illustrate the flexibility of BAAKFIL typologies in the Tool-kit, the project includes a compact universal unit for active seniors, a smaller unit with a rental suite and a larger unit with a neighbourhood commercial hair salon. The project illustrates the range of BAAKFIL unit sizes from 600sf to 1700sf (55–158sm) and densities from 22.7 to 31.8 units/acre (56–79.5 units/ha).This project is also the subject of Chapter 6.3 Narrative: Design Fiction. The landowner is considering construction, designed as per the condominium business model, in 2024.

Demonstration Project No.2

This is a rental project for a developer on a site of 6500sf (600sm). It is an existing one-and-a-half storey 1950s' house with a new two level universal unit and one larger unit with rental suite and carport. At 26 units/acre (65 units/ha), it examines the new zoning bylaws in Edmonton to be implemented in January 2024. A Development Permit is pending. The site is a 45x145 foot (14m x 44.2m) corner lot in Spruce Avenue, a similar mature neighbourhood to Dovercourt; actually located one block north of the missing middle design competition site referred to by KI*_8 in Chapter 4.2. Kingsway Mall, NAIT campus, hospitals and LRT are within walking distance.

Demonstration Project No. 1

The existing house is in the corner of an L-shaped street in the neighbourhood, on a pie lot with a narrow frontage and back alley. Mature deciduous and conifer trees exist at the lot lines.

The property is typical of mature Edmonton neighbourhoods. The house betrays many of the generic design characteristics of early 1950–1960 subdivisions. The living room faces the street, while the kitchen, bathroom and one bedroom face the backyard. There is no relationship between the house and its site. Headlights shine into the living room at night and, aside from the kitchen window and an after-market deck built sometime after the house is completed, there is no meaningful engagement with the larger backyard. It is as a result, largely unused and, aside from a derelict garage, empty.

Houses on the block have backyard decks, extra living space, front or rear porches. The majority of lots in the neighbourhood are 130–150 feet (40–45m) deep and as a result, garages where they exist, front onto the alley and are most often used for storage. This is because it is more convenient to park on the street and bring groceries or guests into the house when it is a shorter walking distance. It is not uncommon to see snow build up through the winter on backyard driveways.

In these neighbourhoods, the orientation of a unit does not factor into its layout. Living space always faces the street, and as a result some see the sun while others do not. Over time, property

▲ Figure 6.1.1

Existing site

value adjusts to recognize that a sunny, wind-protected backyard is more desirable, but this is never a factor laying out the efficient road and alley networks of neighbourhoods at the time.

The landowner plans to refinish the basement, refurbish the kitchen and main floor bathroom and add a small entry porch to the front of the house.

There is a new addition of a media room that faces the trellis between the house and the universal unit.

▲ Figure 6.1.2

BAAKFIL

▼ Figure 6.1.3

Street front

This is the setting for BAAKFIL, a new condominium. It fits into the typical mature neighbourhood that is a permeable, walkable grid system. North–south or east–west lot axes are generally easy to work with to enhance the orientation to sun and wind with new renovations, additions or development. This contrasts with the more pragmatic, land efficient newer subdivisions at the outer edges of the city, with cul de sacs and crescents that ignore the grid system. Mature trees and sidewalks are compelling and proximity to services retains property value yielding a predictably desirable neighbourhood.

As a bare land condominium, the property for the BAAKFIL project is not subdivided. Common area in back is shared. As a micro-community, it shares common values as well as land. The condominium corporation assumes responsibility for the common area upkeep. The corporation is self-governing, enabling group discussion and decision making typical for small condo corporations. The original owner remains in place while underused land includes mixed use and multigenerational living. This is a prototype BAAKFIL model oriented to the landowner's family and friends.

The *parti* includes a universal unit, a smaller unit with a rental suite and a larger unit with a neighbourhood commercial hair salon at the lower level. The existing house kitchen window flanks the axis for a linear trellis, from which each unit is accessible with a porch or a lower terrace. This defines a linear courtyard including a communal garden, an existing apple tree and parking at the alley. The composition provides spatial privacy and a village-like sense of place with the scale of the units increasingly higher toward the alley, more distant from the existing adjacent houses. *The entire development is not visible from the street and there is more space between BAAKFIL units than between the existing neighbour houses.* Only two diseased trees at the alley have been removed for the parking area, while others are limbed.

Legend

1 Parking
2 Trellis walkway
3 Lane Unit
4 Court Unit
5 Universal Unit
6 House
7 Lower Terrace
8 Deck
9 Roof Garden
10 House Addition
11 Garden
12 Salon
13 Rental Suite
14 Porch
15 Apple tree

▲ Figure 6.1.4

Site Plan

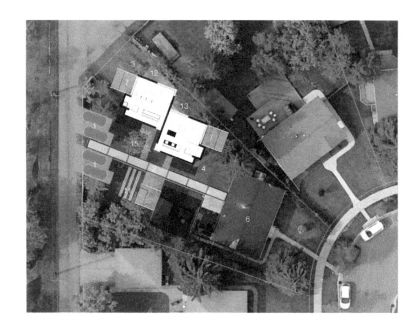

Legend

1 Parking
2 Trellis walkway
3 Lane Unit
4 Court Unit
5 Universal Unit
6 House
7 Lower Terrace
8 Deck
9 Roof Garden
10 House Addition
11 Garden
12 Salon
13 Rental Suite
14 Porch
15 Apple tree

▲ Figure 6.1.5

Lower Level

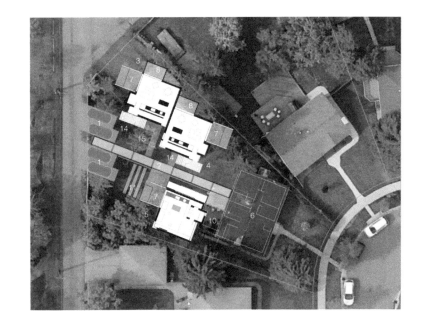

Legend

1   Parking
2   Trellis walkway
3   Lane Unit
4   Court Unit
5   Universal Unit
6   House
7   Lower Terrace
8   Deck
9   Roof Garden
10 House Addition
11 Garden
12 Salon
13 Rental Suite
14 Porch
15 Apple tree

▲ Figure 6.1.6

Main Level

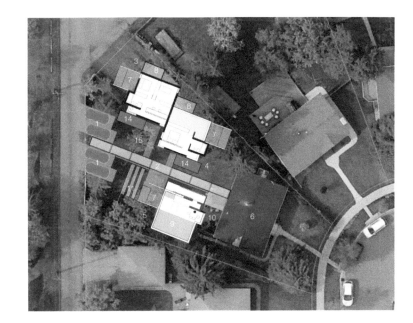

Legend

1   Parking
2   Trellis walkway
3   Lane Unit
4   Court Unit
5   Universal Unit
6   House
7   Lower Terrace
8   Deck
9   Roof Garden
10 House Addition
11 Garden
12 Salon
13 Rental Suite
14 Porch
15 Apple tree

▲ Figure 6.1.7

Upper Level

▲ Figure 6.1.8

Drone views

▲ Figure 6.1.9

Winter

▲ Figure 6.1.10

Rain Garden

▲ Figure 6.1.11

Trellis

▲ Figure 6.1.12

Porches and garden

▲ Figure 6.1.13

WOONERF

▲ Figure 6.1.14

Sunset

▲ Figure 6.1.15

Gentrified alley frontage

Demonstration Project No.2

This is a rental project for a local developer on a much smaller corner lot. It comprises a small one-and-a-half storey post-war house and two BAAKFIL units—a two-level universal unit and a larger unit with a separate rental suite.

The existing house is retained for the owner with minor renovations to the plan. A courtyard separates the house from the universal unit, designed for a friend of the owner. The larger BAAKFIL unit includes a shared carport (or future garage) at the back alley.

Each unit faces the avenue and while care is taken to afford each its own character, the composition is integrated by the inclusion of a continuous metal trellis that follows the front roof profile of the large BAAKFIL unit, adding privacy to the upper roof deck of the universal unit, defining the ground level courtyard and framing a new verandah at the front of the existing house.

The new city bylaws, to be officially adopted in January 2024, allow this development, since a much higher density than illustrated here is permitted. The low neighbourhood impact with retention of the existing house is a bonus. Only a derelict garage is demolished.

The complex is net zero ready and the quality of finishes is durable although not equal to the pie lot pilot since the difference in the average income profile of the two communities impacts the budget. This development is also smaller than new apartments in the immediate area and elsewhere in the neighbourhood.

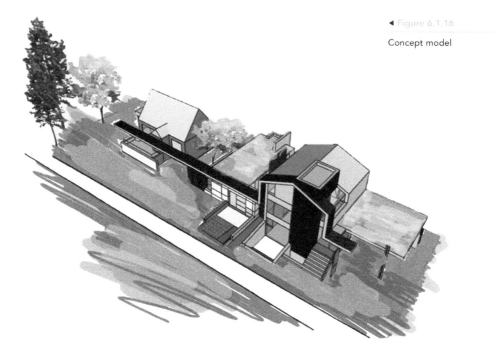

◀ Figure 6.1.16

Concept model

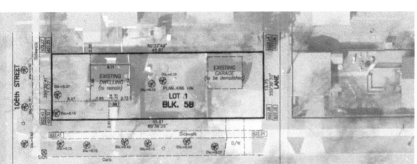

◀ Figure 6.1.17

Plot Plan and existing house

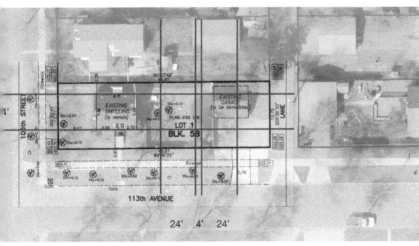

◀ Figure 6.1.18

Setback order

▲ Figure 6.1.19

Site Plan

24'
7200mm

24'
7200mm

Legend

1 Rental Suite
2 Kitchen
3 Living
4 Sleeping
5 Utility
6 Landscaped Terrace
7 Universal Unit
8 Lift
9 Ramp
10 Exterior stair
11 Main Unit
12 Porch
13 Roof Terrace
14 Work
15 Trellis
16 Carport

24'
7200mm

24'
7200mm

24'
7200mm

Legend

1 Rental Suite
2 Kitchen
3 Living
4 Sleeping
5 Utility
6 Landscaped Terrace
7 Universal Unit
8 Lift
9 Ramp
10 Exterior stair
11 Main Unit
12 Porch
13 Roof Terrace
14 Work
15 Trellis
16 Carport

24'
7200mm

24'
7200mm

24'
7200mm

Legend

1 Rental Suite
2 Kitchen
3 Living
4 Sleeping
5 Utility
6 Landscaped Terrace
7 Universal Unit
8 Lift
9 Ramp
10 Exterior stair
11 Main Unit
12 Porch
13 Roof Terrace
14 Work
15 Trellis
16 Carport

▲ Figure 6.1.23a

Street views

▲ Figure 6.1.23b

Street views

CHAPTER 6 Demonstration Projects

▲ Figure 6.1.24

Front elevation

6.2 Evaluation

The second round of key informant interviews involves a peer review and this second 'bookend' event occurs during August–October 2022 when the creative project is about 80% complete. Interviews at this juncture are framed around the evaluation of a prior, preliminary submission sent to the Key Informants:

The Business Model
The Design Tool-kit
The Demonstration Project
Design Fiction Video Narrative (Symposium June 2022).

> The idea of finding a way for landowners sitting on wealth they can't use to invest in the development and in their neighbourhood at the same time is spot on. We don't need huge housing and downsizing maintenance is a bonus.
>
> KI_6

The submission introduces the acronym BAAKFIL to the Key Informants. This series of interviews does not use specific questions to launch a discussion. Instead, Key Informants are asked to comment on the work. The feedback proves helpful to determine a pathway for additional needed work and remains focused on the scope of the research objective whilst not wandering from the topic.

The second round of recorded interviews sees a positive response to BAAKFIL while at the same time asking for more. I review these matters in this chapter. The business model addresses the research question, supported by the BAAKFIL Design Tool-kit that connects respect to densification.

The major takeaway from every participant is consensus that land cost removal or mitigation is the 'break through' to innovation and new knowledge in the business plan. The land issue is the key to addressing the scope of the research inquiry.

The word 'respect' is interpreted throughout the exhibited work. Again, every Key Informant supports the idea of 'respect'.

KI_1, KI_2, KI_3 and KI_6 each agree with my claim that bylaw reform—introduced in many urban jurisdictions since the first round of interviews—will inevitably see land prices continue to increase in single family neighbourhoods. Existing single house lots can now be replaced with infill in the form of multi-storey apartments. This is clearly a goal in Edmonton based on its impending new bylaw and City Plan that aspires to densities of 42 units/acre (105 units/ha). I now claim this a developer 'entitlement' bylaw that will do more to exacerbate the impact of infill and densification in mature urban neighbourhoods if it becomes a multi-city movement. KI_1, KI_ 6 and KI*_8 agree this will not advance the creation of affordable housing with increased land cost. Here we see pressure from the larger development companies that claim increased affordability results from increasing the supply of much higher density, multi-floor walk-up apartments.

The spectre of allowing eight dwellings or an apartment block on the pie lot demonstration project, for example, is deemed untenable to the neighbourhood from a respect and a social justice perspective.

All agree that BAAKFIL changes this narrative.

Ground-oriented, flexible housing typologies make housing more affordable by removing land cost from the developer proforma. The business model and Design Tool-kit support retention of existing serviceable housing, addressing the climate change agenda while maintaining neighbourhood character. It incentivizes neighbourhood landowners to have a say in the maintenance and growth of their communities at the same time. New BAAKFIL units can be designed as custom builds. These types of comments are many.

KI_6 claims that while cities struggle to think differently about housing affordability and what it means, BAAKFIL also revives the concept of the living back alley (per KI_1) and contributes to the city.

KI_2 claims the BAAKFIL business model may be impacted but could also be impervious to inflation since land cost is removed from the proforma equation. BAAKFIL will always be less costly than alternative models that incorporate land cost into the project proforma.

The work crosses theory and practice. It investigates how to make respectful densification happen which is of utmost importance. Sprawl has not been good to us with its climate change and social inequity challenges. It is important to see the combination of new knowledge and experience in your work where you say 'let me show you what can be done and how it can be done'. We need this and we need this fast.

KI_1

KI_1 suggests the definition of what constitutes affordable housing will continue to change due to rising interest rates and other costs, but BAAKFIL housing is more affordable regardless, with land cost removed from the proforma. Removal of land cost and retention of existing serviceable housing is a permanent formula. In addition, the key informant review salutes the retention of existing housing, lower land maintenance, shared responsibilities and downsizing of units as promoted in the BAAKFIL Design Tool-kit. KI_5 and KI_2 ask how I intend to spread the message?

We should not disrupt the social fabric of old neighbourhoods with big density. Building neighbourhood buy-in first will kill NIMBY.

KI_7

You are ticking a lot of the right boxes—climate, community, social, infrastructure, cities, and especially affordability.

Can you tick some more?

And, how are you going to get this idea out there?

KI_2

Other considerations for remedial work are:

1. Re-evaluate zoning reform with currency of BAAKFIL. Does BAAKFIL fit within the rewriting of municipal regulations and zoning reform initiated in several cities during the research cycle?
2. The business model needs to be considered for alternate housing models. A *rental* scenario or leasing as well as for *sales*. Can you de-commodify housing while de-linking it from home ownership? There needs to be more focus on this if rental housing as 'home' is going to increase as a result of continued high cost.
3. KI_3 is particularly interested in investigating other forms of land acquisition through land leases, trusts, co-ops and potential leveraging of municipal owned land.
4. KI_1 and KI_6 and interestingly KI*_9 ask why just pie lots? Can BAAKFIL be shown to work in ALL lot configurations?
5. KI_5 asks if the flexibility of BAAKFIL is adaptable to other locations than just the mature neighbourhood in the business model and in the Tool-kit?
6. KI_2 recommends not re-thinking every aspect of risk. Work within the industry by staying in its lane.
7. KI_1 believes reviving the alley is important for city making.
8. KI_2 and KI_5 are adamant this is an easily extendable proposition. Can you spend more time thinking about the possibilities beyond the mature neighbourhood, e.g. suburbia? Can you also expand the business plan to for, example, examine BAAKFIL as a possible solution to overextended mortgages? Given the advent of Air BnB is this an applicable model as well?

Gentle densification and respect. I hope this helps people reckon with the scale of change needed in our cities.

KI_2

My reflections after this round of interviews yield serious impacts and result in some major changes, now fully incorporated into the entirety of Chapters 4, 5 and 6. These final key informant interviews also coincide with discussions held with others in my CoP at an early date in 2022, enabling sufficient time to expand the research, develop Demonstration Project No. 2, broaden the impact of the objectives and complete a more fulsome development of the BAAKFIL paradigm.

I address several topics:

1. Zoning reform analysis is updated.
2. The business model includes both rental and sales options. There are now two demonstration projects that address previous Items 2 and 3—the original pie lot pilot (including a detailed project proforma) and a rental project on a corner lot. The Design Tool-kit addresses these scenarios as well, alongside the critical inclusion of universal design, in response to the aging demographic.
3. Item 7 is developed only conceptually in context with the question.

Given the timing of the interviews, some of this new work is presented in the November 2022 Symposium.

Chapter 7 Conclusion addresses remaining matters such as the NORC (New York State Office for the Aging, 2022) and WOONERF (Natures Path, 2022), including a reflection on the scope of work.

6.3 Narrative: Design Fiction—Living with BAAKFIL

The pie lot pilot Demonstration Project No. 1 in Chapter 6.1 is further explored through a fictional narrative that imagines a consumer tour of the completed project with a new BAAKFIL owner. To do this, we fast forward five years to capture the intersection of community value sets with the aspirations of BAAKFIL.

The written narrative is modified from the original video presentation to include images so it can stand alone.

At the end of the original presentation I muse about my role as an architect. These questions are further explored as a reflection at the end of the narrative.

The original presentation can be viewed at http://bjalstudio.ca/baakfil/

Welcome to what has become for us an exercise of 'baby boomer' downsizing. We purged a lot of our belongings that the family didn't want, but with a separate work studio and roof deck, a large kitchen, compact living space, trees, small yard and sunshine everywhere—it's a delightful and very energy efficient place to live.

Pie lot pilot

Like a lot of houses in the neighbourhood—we have a porch in the trees; but ours is on the roof! It overlooks the garden and is very private. We walk past that old apple tree over there every day, when we come back from our many walks along our neighbourhood alleys with our little puppy dog.

Our daughter lives in the original house. She and her husband have worked from home since Covid-19, so they have become eyes on the street. She and her Mom are very close, so it was an easy decision for us to move to their property. The roof porch off the studio has become the morning coffee place for them during the warmer months—instead of starting the day with an email or a text. Our grand-daughter is their only child and she is away at university and plans to stay in Calgary when she graduates. She remains a kid at heart and likes to stay with us in the roof studio when she is in the city so she can use our indoor lift. It is also useful for bringing food and drinks back and forth. Hopefully we will be fortunate enough to never need it for its real purpose as a wheelchair conveyance.

The kids did some work in the house with their share of the proceeds of selling these three BAAKFIL units as well as paying off what was left of their mortgage. They love the neighbourhood and plan to stay. This has worked out well for us too. We bought our unit well below infill rates and we don't need to look after the yard. We take turns tending the garden and shovelling snow in the winter.

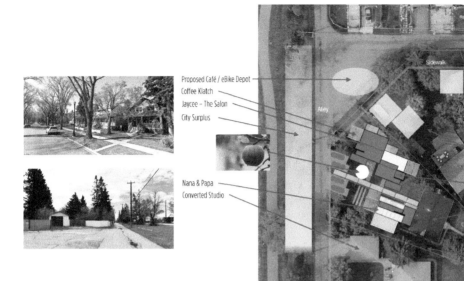

Proposed Café / eBike Depot
Coffee Klatch
Jaycee – The Salon
City Surplus

Nana & Papa
Converted Studio

Sidewalk

Alley

Thinking
Ricardo & Maria
Daughter & Son in Law

No Fence!

Street

▲ Figure 6.3.2

Site Plan

Our harvest includes some of the best cooking apples around. That apple tree is 60 years old and is the centrepiece of the trellised courtyard. Our apple pie block party every fall is a great pot-luck feast and we set long tables for 40 people under the trellis, but I digress.

On the other side of us are two more units, and each was designed by the architect with a lower suite. They are bigger than ours. The smaller one has a roof garden and an interior hydroponic vertical garden incorporated around the inside stair. Ricardo and Maria are immigrants from Brazil. Ricardo met our daughter through work. They are crazy gardeners and while they are both eligible for their Canadian citizenship next year, they are teaching us all things Portuguese.

Jaycee lives in the unit by the alley with her engineer husband. Her Mom is in her sixties and used to live in an apartment building in the neighbourhood but now she rents Ricardo and Maria's lower suite. Strange maybe, but this is because Jaycee runs her little hair salon out of her own lower suite off the back alley. Ricardo and Maria can off-set their mortgage payments every month while Jaycee's Mom lives close by—but not too close! Jaycee gives a discount to the neighbourhood, so she is super busy all the time with new customers alongside her regular clientele. Her salon has a commercial coffee maker, so we helped her set up a little coffee klatch on the weekends when her patio is open for business—just like a mini Parisienne café. We have cappuccinos over there as the morning sun swings around and we just hang out reading the news on our iPads while others get their hair cut. Jaycee does the little kids on Saturday mornings, so this has turned into a bit of a gathering place for the younger parents in the neighbourhood.

We have a closely knit, multifaceted micro-community here on site with seniors, young people and even a small neighbourhood business. We live independently, have lots of privacy but still see each other if only to say hello it seems, every day.

Our enclave is very energy efficient too. The architect calls those glass things over there on two of the units our photovoltaic solar panels. The original house has solar panels on the roof too. There are earth tubes under the ground that draw cool fresh air into each unit so we don't need air conditioning in the hot summer. We are close to net zero energy use. We have had to learn a new way of using buildings to take advantage of all the features to keep our carbon footprint low. But with lots of insulation, water miser fixtures, collecting rainwater to use along with recycling our grey water to flush our toilets, for irrigation and to wash the car; we are getting smarter. We all share the energy that is created on the property together. Not every unit has the panels. We are in the trees so we have too much shadow and the original house of course is not as efficient despite what they have done with new windows and higher efficiency heating systems. The architect calls this sharing strategy a type of regeneration. He claims that because of

▲ Figure 6.3.3

BAAKFIL Micro Community

this—the shared garden and our community oriented lifestyle where we basically have everything we need—we live in a one minute city!

Last year the city paved a new sidewalk down one side of the alley—the cost is included in our neighbourhood improvement levy. The community league is planning to develop that unused triangle of land behind us that the city will lease to them to build a real café, ebike and scooter depot next year.

This little enclave of the neighbourhood is quite active now, whereas before it was a problem space with derelict garages, messy yards and the odd break-in.

All of a sudden, the alley is a convivial skinny street. It is not unusual when we walk the dog, to see the kids selling lemonade, people rebuilding their fences—using them as planters or bee hotels.

So far there are four BAAKFIL projects on this block alone and the immediate neighbours are thinking about it now too. There is an idea emerging on the other corner at the end of the block about contriving a NORC. The neighbours are co-operating with a new BAAKFIL proposal landowner to take the next step in designing their own 'natural' occurring retirement community. It used to be that everyone was against development of any kind here and that sure has changed.

It's happening! What is interesting is that people are not fussed about this densification agenda. When it comes to new developments, owners take turns sitting on the Community League Design Panel. We are allowed to review new developments

▼ Figure 6.3.4

BAAKFIL trellis backyard and garden block party

as they are proposed. We aren't architects or planners so all we really want to see is that it is a good fit. We now feel we have a say in building the neighbourhood and its pride of place.

Being close to transit and shopping and our leafy streetscapes makes it attractive for people to come here. For those who have lived here for ages, they are not threatened. They feel safer. For example, we agreed with our neighbour to tear down the old fence on the property line and not replace it. Both properties now feel larger and we each see more of the existing trees. The Community League has renewed credibility with the city too. The city understands we are helping them since they are no longer getting complaints all the time.

This pie lot was a pilot demonstration project that works with the new city bylaws. The trees were kept, the house was kept, none of these new units are higher than the existing houses down the block and their footprint is no bigger than a two-car garage. You can't even see this development from the street.

The proposal was not controversial as a result. It was a welcome relief compared to those many residents who now must live next door to the three-storey infills that pepper so many mature neighbourhoods. BAAKFIL is catching on—for all age groups and newcomers.

It has a better long-term impact on the densification agenda when projects are approved because they respect the neighbourhood. This also very importantly gives agency to

▲ Figure 6.3.5

BAAKFIL just visible above right window

residents—and the community now self organizes at the local level of rule-making, like the NORC proposal, rather than being governed previously by old zoning.

The City has surplus land across the alley. We are working to have it leased to the Community League for development. There is some exciting talk of a housing design competition.

BAAKFIL is more affordable as a ground-oriented missing middle housing choice. The units are a bit smaller, but then again, so are our households—and the market is responding in various ways.

Residents are incentivized to improve their properties, even if they are not developed. For instance, our neighbour just cleaned out his garage and built a pottery studio for his wife. She is there all the time and can show and sell her work off the alley.

What really is the best about this model though, is existing owners are not displaced and their houses are not torn down. They aren't being pushed out by infill or apartment buildings. Moreover, the alleys are getting sidewalks, BAAKFIL units now have their own addresses, land is better utilized, communities are safer and, in places, much more active. This has happened with more flexible zoning, in less than five years.

It's funny to think about it—but our architect reminds us this is how the prairie city started in the first place—without zoning bylaws. Family, friends and newcomers all lived together, neighbourhoods were walkable with mixed use services at the end of every block with housing above stores, permeable streets and easy access to what would eventually become our downtown. Of course, it was much smaller then, but the principles are exactly the same.

We hear urban designers and indeed politicians promoting a new, innovative idea of the 15 minute city—but that's what it was.

The narrative speculates on a number of things but is realistic. The Edmonton Federation of Community Leagues (EFCL) endorses the community support framework inherent to the narrative. Alongside EFCL staff, I also meet and promote these ideas to the City of Edmonton Urban Planning Committee and the bylaw renewal team

Today, the City is implementing its land use and zoning bylaws to incorporate a more moderate review of building proposals to increase building supply. Unfortunately, community concerns are not evident beyond that. This narrative, however, is didactic. It takes the position that responsible, respectful design and community building has room within the new bylaws to offer an engaging look at community growth when seen through a different lens. Our message is being heard.

I have declared that we will not densify our way out of the housing crisis. Density itself may not even be the issue if done respectfully. BAAKFIL as an alternative will certainly be more dense than infill as we know it. Does this matter if it can be transformative and if communities with their neighbourhoods support it?

Respect, in a much broader context, must also be about our humanity in making cities.

George Baird in his *Writings on Architecture and the City* (2015) posits the 'lot' as the basis of urban morphology. I realize that the problem of housing densification in cities—is really more about the rather hostile environments that are created because of the 'lot' today, driven by laws, regulation, greed and antipathy towards others. All things that need to be fixed.

To me the narrative has significant meaning when neighbours agree to not replace a simple worn-out fence between their properties. This speaks subliminally to the idea of community connection. In our real life, there is no fence separating our lakefront cottage from our neighbours. A fence is anti-social to the spirit of living in the country where we say hello, help one another, share a fire in the evenings or a BBQ on weekend afternoons. Why have a fence in the city if neighbours decide to come together?

New subdivision development precludes this discussion. Construction of fences begins at the same time as the roads and services, well before houses are built. Territory is quickly defined on titled lots.

▲ Figure 6.3.6

The fence

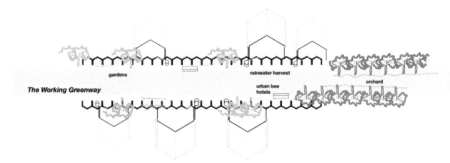

▲ Figure 6.3.7

The working greenway

The notion of territory and the perception of privacy and perhaps safety is wrongly embedded in a psyche that predetermines the need for separation. This is one more manifestation of the lot as counter-productive to community and a good test of George Baird's argument.

At the beginning of the research, one of our introductory exercises examines contextual relationships around the everyday. In other words, to see. We take numerous random photographs of our immediate environs in a short period of time; then analyse the results.

I re-discover the fence—instead of a privacy mechanism—as a catalyst to some hidden prospect instead. I find value in the idea of a working greenway, with fences running parallel to the public realm to yield other possible uses. Can BAAKFIL in this sense work in parallel with the alleys in the city?

Can it promote a greater sense of being together and dilute the territorial necessities?

Can BAAKFIL represent a better idea of community?

I have already concluded that communities need more autonomy to self-organize. In dissecting its parts, the 'lot' morphology through a more ethical framework may help us find a deeper narrative about making respectful places in the city.

References

Baird, G. (2015). *Writings on architecture and the city*. London: Artiface Books on Architecture.

Natures Path. (2022, November). https://naturespath.com/en-ca/blogs/posts/woonerf-the-dutch-solution-to-city-planning

New York State Office for the Aging. (2022, November). NORC. https://aging.ny.gov/naturally-occurring-retirement-community-norc

7.1 Conclusion

This chapter reflects upon the findings of the research with my Key Informants and includes a self-evaluation of BAAKFIL.

I first discuss whether BAAKFIL can be considered an innovation. This is a personal reflection about my own quest for new knowledge.

Next, I provide an overview analysis of BAAKFIL relative to my research objective, using the acronym for BAAKFIL as a framework. I address the research question in the same manner. Two simple graphs map these ideas.

This chapter also explains the challenges I receive from my Key Informants to take BAAKFIL to another level. In total, I provide a personal reflection of the whole, to summarize the conclusions for each chapter.

I close with an observation about BAAKFIL and its potential.

Innovation Defined

Within the context of doctoral research and the development of new knowledge, can BAAKFIL be considered an innovation?

BAAKFIL is unique, but it is intended to fit inside an existing system rather than transform it altogether. This book argues that, while the housing industry is constipated by its own reluctance to rethink the market (largely because it doesn't have to), there is room for innovation inside the system that can challenge the status quo and really focus on the primary needs of the consumer—affordability, choice and adaptability.

The idea of housing innovation however—to most architects—conjures historic moments in the annals of contemporary multi-unit family design. Good examples are Le Corbusier's Unité D'Habitation in Marseille, France and the Villa Savoye outside Paris; and in North America, Rudolf Schindler's Kings Road house in Los Angeles. All three share, among other things, iconic roof terraces that are deeply influential moments in the context of 20th-century Modernism. Moshe Safdie's Habitat '67 in Montreal takes the idea of a roof garden even further, positioning its creator as one of the best recognized architects in the world.

It is interesting to compare these models—L'Unité especially, built around multiple iterations throughout Europe to establish an alternate living option at societal scale. Schindler experiments with ideas about co-habitation and tilt-up concrete construction and it remains an early one-off of its time. Habitat, despite its total uniqueness (and waiting list even today to get in), and its manifestation of Safdie's lifelong pursuit of 'for everyone a garden', enjoys limited success elsewhere. Its cost and complex organization, originally envisioned as a prototype that could be built in a factory and mass produced for

     DOI: 10.4324/9781003414803-7

▲ Figure 7.1.1

Roof Terrace, Ville Savoye

distribution around the globe, arrives too early and is deemed too adventurous to be reasonable at the time. It is unfortunately largely dismissed as a novelty.

To most architects, however, would not these sample iconic projects define the big idea of housing innovation—outside of the established systems and industries—against which any new idea about housing must be compared?

The Merriam-Webster dictionary defines innovation as 'a new idea, method or device' or, the 'introduction of something new or different'. Innovation therefore is seen as something entirely new or a change made to an existing product, idea or field. By comparison, an invention—a term not used frequently by architects—is a device, or a process originated after study or experiment. The common telephone is a good example of both.

The original telephone is an invention. It did not exist previously and transforms communication. The mobile phone makes this idea of communication portable, thus an invention and an innovation given its purpose and use. The smart phone is an innovation. It is something new, taking the original idea into a range of new possibilities as a computer in one's hand.

Habitat '67 (courtesy Professor
David Covo, McGill University)

▼ Figure 7.1.3

The phone as innovation

In this context, this book claims BAAKFIL as an innovation of *ways* and innovation of *things*:

The BAAKFIL business model can be deployed via conventional financing instruments, i.e. the use of land as collateral. It is an innovation of *ways*, since the land is not purchased by the developer and its actual cost—regardless of location or market forces—is removed from a project proforma since the landowner retains tenure in the property rather than selling it completely. It is innovative, since this can apply across the country and be done by any landowner at any time. This is, as a result, a scalable societal business model that can impact the housing market from within the system to increase affordability. The business model is something entirely new.

The innovation of *things* is found where any house builder can construct BAAKFIL using conventional construction methods. Bespoke design can be incorporated by following the principles of the BAAKFIL Design Tool-kit to address basic criteria of site orientation, sun, wind protection and views, while enabling new technologies to be incorporated with flexible and compact layouts.

The BAAKFIL Design Tool-kit does not aspire to the unique spectacularization of a Unité or a Habitat; but it does contribute to new knowledge by envisioning a systems organizational framework that can be deployed, within the industry across the country. This is change made to an existing product, idea or field.

The research objective is satisfied as shown in Table 7.1.1.

I start with the housing question. The affordability crisis is reduced to a limited conversation about supply and density. This also leaves things missing about community. I conclude the housing question must include the idea of house as home. Table 7.1.2 takes the objectives into the research question and demonstrates the

▶ Table 7.1.1

BAAKFIL as an acronym

Back	BAAKFIL uses 'found' land fronting onto a back alley. This is the key to the business model.
Alley	The back alley is gentrified with addresses, a sidewalk and gentle neighbourhood densification.
Advantage	Smaller properties are available within fractionalized titled lots and sold at lower rates, increasing affordability.
Kinship	Housing for community supports friends, relatives or immediate family, newcomers and the open market.
Family	Families can live closer to one another, together or independently.
Integrated	The Design Tool-kit integrates new typologies to enable a self-governing micro-community on a lot, or lots.
Living	The Design Tool-kit addresses the 2022 Canadian Census of smaller households and is inclusive for all ages.

societal impacts of BAAKFIL, starting with mitigating and eliminating land cost.

The research objective is also satisfied through the Research Question as in Table 7.1.2.

◀ Table 7.1.2

How can my practice deliver	The practice is re-constituted into a new development company to deliver BAAKFIL consulting services.
Sustainable	Experience in practice with sustainable design performance metrics is reflected in the Design Tool-kit.
Densification	The BAAKFIL business model incorporates retention of an existing house and new ground-oriented typologies on site.
Options	A Design Tool-kit offers adaptable typologies based on a 24x24 double car garage footprint.
that address Attainability	The business model retains existing housing and leverages land equity for new development on 'found' land.
Affordability	Affordability is predicated on removing land cost from the developer proforma and mitigating consumer land cost.
Demographics	The Design Tool-kit addresses all age groups and family structures including universal design for seniors to thrive.
Bespoke needs	The Design Tool-kit is based on modular consistency, an infrastructure core and enables flexible unit design.
Societal expectations	BAAKFIL responds to aging in community, kinship values of family, multigenerational and intergenerational living.
and is Respectful	BAAKFIL integrates neighbourhood scale, context and alleys without altering the existing streetscape.
to Place?	BAAKFIL fits into mature neighbourhoods across Canada; responsive to site and local conditions.

Research Question

Reflection

BAAKFIL is a housing model that increases affordability by removing land cost and promoting respectful densification. It is accepted by Key Informants and my CoP cohort as a welcome innovation within the housing industry. It is a contribution to new knowledge.

The second round of key informant interviews is focused more on expanding the possibilities of BAAKFIL, rather than dissecting its parts. Accordingly, I need to reflect upon what is possible and what I determine to be outside of the scope of the research inquiry.

The dominant objective and scope of the research is based on the discovery that the housing question is best answered for me by a new approach to the availability and the cost of land. This ultimately drives the research objective, the research question, the evolution of BAAKFIL and constitutes the bulk of the work.

Other ideas from my Key Informants are deemed valuable and worthy of more study. Given the timing of the second round of interviews, I am able to reflect on and incorporate the relevant input into the work. However, I situate other observations as I describe in this chapter outside of my scope of work for this dissertation. I finally reflect upon the 'art of the possible' for BAAKFIL.

Chapter 1 Introduction

The impact of BAAKFIL on my practice is profound. I start a new company called BAAKFIL Developments Ltd. in January 2023 to provide future consulting services and promotional communications to industry and the profession. This transition away from my traditional practice of architecture is expected to include development of BAAKFIL projects including those in this book.

I think about future digital iterations of the BAAKFIL Design Tool-kit as an app or AI that architects, builders and consumers can use. Digital assist apps are already found in the industry for site planning and stock house plans. The rise of AI brings with it many opportunities and challenges. In the right hands, AI algorithms might, for example, source site suitability across the country or even bespoke design as the next iteration of BAAKFIL—a Design Tool-kit 2.0.

Key Informants encourage me to expand the scope of the work to investigate BAAKFIL beyond the mature neighbourhood. This is a significant challenge for the future.

Chapter 2 The Problem

Context

The context of the research pivots after completing an analysis of zoning reform. Originally I did identify this as one of the biggest barriers to the housing question. Now municipalities in Canada since 2020 are changing their approach increasingly towards flexibility—much needed to supersede outdated zoning bylaws.

What I see emerging however is what I am calling a developer entitlement zoning model. The need to increase supply to address the housing crisis is paramount with government today. This means that zoning barriers must be overcome or removed so developers can quickly mobilize. Many municipalities support this idea. I discuss the implications of aggressive densities and much larger projects that The City of Edmonton is now planning to approve for single family neighbourhoods with its new zoning bylaws. I conclude this is a negative decision based on the increased scale of multi-unit projects (one of our AST stakeholders calls them 'pop-up' apartments) that can be approved without consultation.

This poses another wicked problem to address with zoning renewal; but BAAKFIL is largely unaffected by this. Zoning reform is now less of a barrier to BAAKFIL. One might claim this circumstance is a windfall for the acceptance of BAAKFIL. As a gentle approach to densification and new relaxed zoning, the concept is compliant. Finally, as a respectful alternative typology to begin with, BAAKFIL enjoys support from community leagues and the public already exposed to the idea in Edmonton thus far.

It remains to be seen what transpires as regulations are increasingly relaxed. Toronto City Council now approves multiplexes (up to four units on a single lot) across the city to address the growing housing crisis. This is surprisingly announced in early May 2023 (City News, 2023). Long seen as a bastion of restrictive zoning, especially in the Yellowbelt areas, the city typically promotes densification in its already heavily populated areas with mid-rise and high-rise apartments. While this new policy is significant, it remains to be studied as to whether affordability will be improved by this introduction of the missing middle in the city. (Again, the discussion is centred around increasing supply. I cannot find any policy framework that compares land cost to affordability). Barely one week after this announcement, the Canadian Real Estate Association announces that the average selling price of a home on its MLS system in April at $716,000 is an increase of more than $100,000 since January 2023 (Evans, P. 2023).

In the coming years, it may prove worthwhile to measure the impact of zoning reform in Canada.

Objective—It Is All About Land

The Key Informant discussions, especially during the first round of interviews, help me to appreciate the housing industry and its inherent barriers to innovation. This research fades, however, when the work finally yields what becomes the core idea of this dissertation— mitigating land cost.

The big idea of appropriation of a small land parcel to another party within a titled lot emerges as the major breakthrough. This is now being referred to as the 'fractionalization' of land.

Methodology—Key Informants

The methodology of key informant interviews to drive the advancement of new knowledge deserves reflection. My extensive Community of Practice, including individuals listed as a KI* in the thesis, provide added value to the discourse. Declining to participate under the normal IRISS protocols for business and personal reasons despite keen interest in the work, their input is significant. Since I follow the Key Informant interview process with them, except that I meet with them on several occasions, I claim them as (qualified) Key Informants, nonetheless. The learnings from interactions with bankers, one developer and one client attest to this claim; especially given how this informs the business model. The semi-structured recorded interviews, transcript process and peer reviews with the IRISS Key Informants stand alone as previously discussed. Both the KI and the KI* prove indispensable to the research.

Chapter 3 BAAKFIL

The evolution of BAAKFIL is rewarding once the topic of land cost mitigation finds its way into the solution space. The discovery that my problem space is all about land cost and what to do about it as a wicked problem, is the moment that changes everything. I discover that addressing land cost is the key to addressing affordability.

From here, I discern that retention of existing serviceable housing stock (versus demolition in favour of infill) is not only connected to the affordability equation, it is also key to maintaining good relations in a neighbourhood. From these two principles, the original research that is compiled into a body of disjointed work and key informant interviews from different experts with different backgrounds, suddenly comes into focus.

Chapter 4 BAAKFIL Business Model

The business model works well for a condominium situation, less so as a rental model. The land in both cases does not need to be subdivided; however, a long term rental strategy works best for the landowner who is interested in cash flow over time, not profit in the short term. The landowner must also be comfortable in partnership with the developer as a joint landlord or, one way or another, buy out the developer or be bought out to re-claim the house. The narrative about this rental model is somewhat opaque, illustrating the complex intersection between a condo and rental scenario. The rental scenario is purposely conflated with a co-op structure as well, to illustrate that a new co-op corporation leaves the landowner one step removed from regaining sole title to the existing house. The implication here is the landowner is willing to completely change the nature of 'ownership' in this context.

Chapter 5 BAAKFIL Design Tool-kit

The design work in the BAAKFIL Tool-kit is decidedly unspectacularized as previously mentioned. This is compared to the context of exaggerated form and surface embellishment found in architectural journals and published projects with the advent of say, parametric design. BAAKFIL is conservative and self-effacing. This is deliberate and, despite my claim the Tool-kit is poised to incorporate other features and thus become as it were, more expressive, it is purposely restrained to ensure the model can exist inside the house building industry, labour driven with imperfect skill sets.

Chapter 6 Demonstration Projects

The two BAAKFIL demonstration projects represent what I call a 'standard tech' response to the marketplace. The work is certainly not 'high tech' and not 'low tech' either (given the sustainability underpinnings of the Tool-kit) but is rather something that is buildable through the housing construction industry. To design BAAKFIL with such restraint is not part of the zeitgeist of my practice and this proves a big challenge to me as a designer, otherwise willing to push comfort levels. But it is DESIGN.

The two BAAKFIL demonstration projects are realistic and there is a possibility that both are realized. This possibility catapults the BAAKFIL business model and Design Tool-kit into a far different world of exposure and evaluation, a true test. This is another reason why BAAKFIL Developments Ltd. exists, in anticipation of more to follow.

Key Informant Interviews

Again, I come to realize my reflection about the Key Informants changes as I analyze the outcomes of the research. The interview process is rich, provocative and I see how this advances my thinking about the housing question generally and BAAKFIL particularly. I speak about this input and how it influences the work in previous chapters. In this section I am left to ponder the 'art of the possible' with them. There are numerous challenges.

I am asked questions about future proofing. Can BAAKFIL survive its second, 25-year cycle—a full generation after its introduction? Is it truly adaptable? Could it, for example, be a solution for the suburbs to repair themselves as Jane Jacobs claims?

Can BAAKFIL be an intergenerational model in a Canadian cultural mosaic likely to become more diverse? By example, can BAAKFIL be modified to become a fully integrated collection of structures on a site or, a collective—sleeping pavilion, living pavilion, eating pavilion, services pavilion? These are compelling ideas for further exploration and while they reside outside the scope of this dissertation, they linger as excellent questions.

I discuss the idea of seniors to thrive and the importance of design for universal living in this regard. Can BAAKFIL be designed as a non-institutional complex? A micro-community—as a *planned* NORC? Naturally organized retirement communities in the context of a BAAKFIL micro-community seems reasonable. Can it be designed to take the idea of a NORC and convert it to smaller scale, medical or care facilities with a similar pavilion orientation as the cited intergenerational example? These are all questions or comments from my Key Informants from which I derive many more. One of my Key Informants tells me that he took the liberty to present the idea of BAAKFIL to one of his clients, the Autistic Inclusive Living Association of Alberta. The concept is well received as a potential assisted living facility for families with adult dependent children. The pie lot demonstration project is now being interrogated beyond the concept stage—this time by the owner who is suddenly interested in providing a universal unit for his aging mother who needs to relocate and may need home care.

These unsolicited and albeit cursory evaluations are fascinating.

Can these ideas about health care fit within a supportive neighbourhood context? An extension of the NORC?

While these possibilities need time for investigation, I am reminded of the BAAKFIL option in the Design Tool-kit whereby neighbours partner *together* with a developer to build a larger cottage court missing middle configuration including more than one existing house, with the same ground-oriented context. This now seems a worthy subject to explore.

With BAAKFIL itself, I am encouraged by two Key Informants (another reason for BAAKFIL Developments Ltd.) to take the core elements of the design parti—i.e. the infrastructure core, and investigate its potential for mass customization and component prefabrication. The issue with prefab modules in the industry today and its higher costs are largely due to transportation costs, highway travel dimension clearances and therefore design limitations and distance from factory to destination. When these factors combine with site assembly that requires a crane and/or temporary relocation or disconnection of overhead powerlines, for example (often a problem with container technology for housing), the economics of prefabrication (i.e. mass production in a controlled environment) are compromised. I now want to explore how kitchens, bathrooms, stairs, pre-wired and pre-plumbed prefabricated service walls can each be plant manufactured (not necessarily in the same facility) and brought to any site on a flatbed truck for efficient assembly without the need for a central 'one stop fits all' factory or infrastructure conflict. I believe this can also be achieved inside the industry.

Finally while I discover the history of the WOONERF in this process, I am intrigued by its application in the discussion of back alley revitalization. Originating in the Netherlands, as an enclave of quiet streets, these are home zones as places where messy, convivial life happens. Children's play, walking, cycling, informal gathering all occur where vehicle speed is controlled and car dominance is reduced. The back alleys of many cities can be reimagined with the WOONERF as a precedent. An important supplement to the BAAKFIL paradigm, I unfortunately only lightly touch upon the potential of this idea in this publication.

I also play with the idea that a WOONERF could actually 'leak' into the upgraded backyards of BAAKFIL and try to expose the implications of this in an illustration found in Chapter 6.1, Figure 6.1.13.

▼ Figure 7.1.4

WOONERF

The Narrative

This book includes three structured narratives. The first is a story about growing up in Montreal that becomes an early reflection on concepts of home. This is written at the beginning of the research while reflecting upon the idea of the housing question. The learnings are highlighted in the essay and influence the entire document. The second is a strategy to filter several overlapping inputs from Key Informants into the business model as single voice compositions. The third is a fictionalized account of the BAAKFIL pie lot demonstration project, fast-forwarded five years to evaluate BAAKFIL intentions and impacts through the eyes of a new resident.

I discover early on how the narrative is a powerful communication methodology and pedagogical tool. It effectively summarizes overlapping ideas from Key Informants and others, while transforming my own historically simple 'analysis, synthesis and evaluation' capacities in practice to one of increased dialogue through storytelling.

BAAKFIL also benefits from this methodology when I use it 'live' as it were; related to controversial topics such as zoning reform and community participation metrics in myriad discussions with government, civic administration and citizen action groups. The idea of a story allays fear and builds a connection with people, using common language around the acceptance of new ideas. Stories expose culture and value sets. As a presentation technique in front of an audience, they can differentiate 'speaking with' from being 'spoken to'. The process can be didactic without being preachy and it can stimulate one's imagination. People try and see themselves inside a narrative; everyone loves a story.

Finally—A Disappointment

In addition to the demonstration projects that test BAAKFIL I organize test beds for BAAKFIL in regions across the country. My thinking is to challenge my CoP architect colleagues (who express keen interest in the idea) and students of architecture (in BAAKFIL design studio charettes) to bring other ideas and local, regional influence into the dissertation.

▼ Figure 7.1.5

BAAKFIL, Kelowna, BC

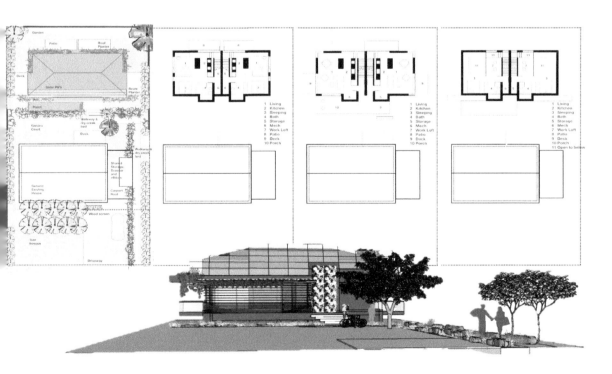

The result is disappointing. Despite some interesting submitted work, the exercise proves too open ended. As volunteers, each is given six months to create the deliverables. Time passes until at the end when personal priorities militate against filing enough submissions. In hindsight, an idea like this—intended as an informal intellectual exploration (and perhaps fun)—needs an honorarium, grant and more rigor to support the expectations. While disappointing, my interest in this regional idea leads me to include one of my own projects that tests BAAKFIL outside the climate context of Alberta.

I close this conclusion chapter with a BAAKFIL proposal for a property with an existing split-level house and carport, but without a back alley, in Kelowna, British Columbia (see Figure 7.1.5). The existing carport becomes a common outdoor threshold that leads to a shared rear courtyard. Two units appear as one building to align with the house, with two additional lower rental units. The project incorporates features that fit the Okanagan context—south facing solar array, rainwater harvesting for the hot gardening months, irrigated vertical living wall of edible greens and storm water capture channel that is otherwise a dry creek landscape bed. (There are no storm sewers in this neighbourhood—everything is surface drained.)

The project is completed for another (local) design competition intended to explore densification in mature neighbourhoods. I again ignore the competition rules that predetermine a specific site and demolish a serviceable house to maximize site density. By keeping the existing house and testing BAAKFIL on the wide (68ft/20.7m) site, I am satisfied that BAAKFIL can be adapted as envisioned in the Design Tool-kit, to many regions across Canada.

References

City News. (2023, May 11). https://toronto.citynews.ca/2023/05/11/toronto-multiplexes-neighbourhoodscitycouncil/#:~:text=Toronto%E2%80%99s%20residential%20landscape%20will%20be%20changing%20in%20an,the%20City%E2%80%99s%20Official%20Plan%20and%20city-wide%20zoning%20bylaw

Evans, P. (2023, May 15). CBC News. cbc.ca/news/business/crea-housing-data-1.6843592

Further Reading

The architect's library is typically filled with volumes and periodicals that span a career. Many address housing in Canada. However few co-relate densification with changing demographics, or land cost as a major constraint to affordability and attainability. These two topics are primary areas of my practice-based research. The following partial list of reference publications in addition to those previously referenced is helpful to the research:

Bozikovic, A. et al., (2019). *House divided: How the missing middle can solve Toronto's affordability crisis. A collection of essays.* Canadiana (print) 20190109645, ebook Coach House Books.

CMHC (1979). National Housing Design Competition 1979—Catalogue winning schemes, ISBN 0–662–50505-0

Correa, C. (2012). *A place in the shade: The new landscape & other essays.* Ostfildern, Germany: Hatje Cantz Verlag. www.hatjecantz.com

Fraker, H. (2013). *The hidden potential of sustainable neighborhoods: Lessons from low-carbon communities.* Washington, DC: Island Press.

Friedman, A. (2006). *The grow home.* Montreal: McGill-Queen's University Press.

Friedman, A. (2015). *A view from the porch.* Montreal: Véhicule Press.

Hwang, V. W., & Horowitt, G. (2012). *The rainforest, the secret to building the next Silicon Valley.* Los Altos Hills, CA: Regenwald.

Jacobs, J. (2004). *Dark age ahead.* Toronto: Random House.

MacLeod, D. (2020). *The architecture of hope.* Kelowna: Wood Lake Publishing.

Moore, C., Allen, G., & Lyndon, D. (2000[1974]). *The place of houses.* Berkeley, CA: University of California Press.

Owen, D. (2009). *Green metropolis: Why living smaller, living closer, and driving less are the keys to sustainability.* New York: Riverhead Books, The Penguin Group.

Parolek, D., with Nelson, A. C. (2020). *Missing middle housing: Thinking big and building small to respond to today's housing crisis.* Washington, DC: Island Press.

Shim, B., Chong, D., Waldheim, C., & Adams, S. (2004). *Site unseen, laneway architecture & urbanism in Toronto.* Toronto: University of Toronto Faculty of Architecture, Landscape and Design.

Author's Notes

The Doctor of Design

The Doctor of Design (DDes) is an advanced practice-based research degree for professionals who wish to build a recognized expertise in a specific topic area and contribute new knowledge to their profession. The structure of the three-year program is focused on a unique practice-based research model. Known as design science research (DSR), this is the methodology used and, in the case of this publication, the foundation for the evolution of BAAKFIL.

DSR is especially suited to architects since it is concerned with change. DSR devises an approach or a prescription for change (i.e. a business plan) and offers solutions (i.e. BAAKFIL) as an artefact that incorporates the prescription, to improve a circumstance (i.e. the housing question) or a situation (i.e. land cost). This is a different approach compared to Natural Sciences Research. Here the concern is how things are and is therefore primarily explanatory in its results.

The Key Informant participant role described throughout this book, distinguishes this methodology. Subject matter experts are chosen and provide input to help establish and/or verify the research context at the beginning of the work. The process culminates in an objective peer review conducted by the same experts as the work is nearing completion, thus closing the circle of inquiry, providing an opportunity for reflection and to then determine what to do next.

In the interim, one's own Community of Practice (COP) enriches the research as these members are comprised of clients, consultants, other professionals, even lay persons (e.g. community groups) who interact regularly with the author on a weekly or in some cases less frequent basis inside or alongside the practice itself.

Together, this enables the creation of new knowledge with influence that goes beyond the traditional study and research process—predicated on analysis of previous research and publications. The reference lists are modest (yet strategic) compared to the much deeper reference or bibliography trajectory of a traditional PhD.

The DDes is particularly suited to BAAKFIL, inasmuch as the topic of land cost is not one that has been traditionally or extensively explored in either natural science research or within the profession of architecture.

The program structure enables students to continue to work within the scope of their own practice, allowing flexible contact within the academy with their supervisory committee. Students participate in Fall and Spring Symposia each year, structured much like a design studio course. Here, in-progress research is shared amongst the cohort while receiving critical feedback from an expert panel of interdisciplinary academics and practitioners (including the supervisory committee). The result is a rich and supportive learning environment and research culture. As part of the first cohort in Canada

DOI: 10.4324/9781003414803-8

for this degree program, I can reflect personally upon this process in addition to that already referenced in the book as follows:

> *The Canadian prairie is a challenging marketplace, where a fiercely independent culture and its relatively young cities have been relatively slow to embrace the larger problems of urban settlements—institutions and governance, housing, transportation, density, and in recent years, of course, the sustainability agenda, social justice, and climate change. As an observer of the world around us but within this prairie context, we have often needed to hold in abeyance many ideas and explorations around architecture and the making of cities in favour of the pragmatics of making a living and working in competition with others in what is now an aging, eroded profession. It has always been a struggle, therefore, but a passion nonetheless to somehow make a difference in practice, despite the myriad challenges we face. The Doctor of Design program at the University of Calgary has opened wide a door often closed to us in this dramatically changing world of practice—the door to new knowledge. It is precisely this newly claimed freedom to research and develop ideas, pursue and entrust them to our practice that is important. In so doing, we can reflect upon our own work and the relevance of new work in this quest, without the constraints of client programs, budgets, schedules and the conservatism that pervades professional life as a service business fraught with risk.*
>
> *In a sense, we become our own client.*
>
> *This freedom yields new energy that is released in the work. We are now at the beginning of a new practice; transformed beyond that of the traditional fee for services 'consultant'. Instead we are now aligned with thought leaders among outside disciplines—pitching ideas and solutions predicated on a deep commitment to both research and design.*
>
> *I see new directional possibilities here for architecture and architects—influencing the making of public policy, bringing our original holistic training to societal issues of the day, and so on. In the end, the overarching goal is to breathe new opportunities into the world of architectural practice and to transmit new knowledge into our communities to nurture positive change. This is neither naïve nor idealistic—it is rather what I am now calling an inclusive, pragmatic optimism and the DDes is the motivational road map to get there.*

The Author

The relevance of my practice to the housing question is exposed in the various chapters of this publication. This section provides

◄ Figure 8.1

Barry Johns

general background about the practice and personal involvement in community and professional service to complete the curriculum vitae.

Barry Johns
    DDes, BArch, Architect, AAA Life Member, FRAIC, (Hon) FAIA, RCA, LEED® AP
    www.bjalstudio.ca
    bjstudio@shaw.ca
    Acadia University, Diploma Architecture/Engineering 1968
    Technical University of Nova Scotia (TUNS)—now Dalhousie University, Bachelor of Architecture 1972
    Alberta Association of Architects Life Member
    Fellow, Royal Architectural Institute of Canada
    Chancellor, College of Fellows, Royal Architectural Institute of Canada (2011–17)
    Director of Practice, Alberta Association of Architects (2015–19)
    Royal Canadian Academy of Arts
    (Honorary) Fellow, American Institute of Architects
    LEED® Accredited Professional
    ORDER Athabasca University (bestowed twice 2013, 2015)
    Doctor of Design 2023

    I am a Canadian Architect in Edmonton, Alberta. I am currently an independent design consultant and mentor. Now retired from an active traditional practice since 1981 and seeking another chapter of lifelong learning, my practice has a history of award winning projects. These can be viewed at www.bjalstudio.ca. Each project is a pursuit of excellence and authenticity, 'treading lightly upon the earth' through environmentally driven, sustainable design. Sustainable architecture and urban design is a fundamental tenet of the practice since the completion of the Edmonton Advanced Technology Centre in 1988.

My early career is deeply connected to Arthur Erickson Architects in Vancouver, British Columbia, as a team member in charge of design and production of the public amenity areas of Robson Square, a North American landmark in architecture and urban design. I am also credited as the design lead and Project Architect for the Evergreen Building in Vancouver completed in 1979, now the first contemporary building in the city to be awarded heritage status.

My interest in Frank Lloyd Wright goes back to my student years. I am active with the Frank Lloyd Wright Foundation and remain a frequent visitor to Taliesin West in Phoenix. I visit and from time to time I am invited to lecture on Frank Lloyd Wright projects in North America. My involvement in the quest to preserve the David and Gladys Wright house in Phoenix when threatened with demolition is part of this experience, including a lecture on the site to the Phoenix Historical League to celebrate its preservation. Living in a world that finally understands the intimate relationship between humankind and the environment, I believe that Wright's philosophy of working in harmony with nature is more relevant today than ever before. In 2018, the American Institute of Architects bestowed me with the Leslie M. Boney Award for outstanding service to the AIA. I am told that this is the first time this prestigious prize has been given to an international member of the AIA.

Practice

My practice as a collaborative studio always engages students and practitioners in an atelier-based culture. In fact, two students of architecture assist me in the DDes work. 'Every decision is a design decision' underpins a teaching practice, including the integration of client, consultant and contractor in the decision-making process. This is an integrated pedagogy across all disciplines about how things are made. Reducing the mystery around the act of design, projects reflect the personality of the circumstance, driven by site, climate, program, culture and social value sets. This is my pursuit of authenticity.

This approach continues to result in invitations to teach and lecture on the work of the practice at Schools of Architecture and conferences across Canada, the USA, Europe and Africa. I also serve on design award juries including the Canada Council, the Prix de Rome and the originally named Moriyama RAIC International Prize. TUNS Press publishes an early monograph on the firm as part of a series on Canadian Architects in 2000 and a downloadable *eBook* is introduced on my website in 2017.

The firm is recognized with more than 100 design awards from around the world, including the Governor General's Medal and an Olympic Gold Medal for the Arts. The practice is published in North America, Britain, Japan and China.

Community Service

The pursuit of authenticity is informed by climate, nature and place. But, above all, architects design for people and in order to do this effectively, we connect with culture and the local condition, especially in rapidly changing urban environments. An example of this importance to me is expressed in the moniker that we attach to the Blatchford Master Plan in The City of Edmonton. The motto is 'connect-i-city' and this is the formative theme in creating a regenerative Masterplan for a community of 25,000 people over 25 years.

This desire to learn about people and their aspirations to inform the work necessitates that everyone in the practice participates in the public realm. For years, I serve on boards and volunteer community groups to advocate for a better quality of life, locally and nationally.

This includes two terms on the Council of the Alberta Association of Architects, the Board of the Downtown Business Association, the Edmonton Urban Design Review Panel, and numerous fundraising boards for the non-profit and philanthropic sectors. For example,

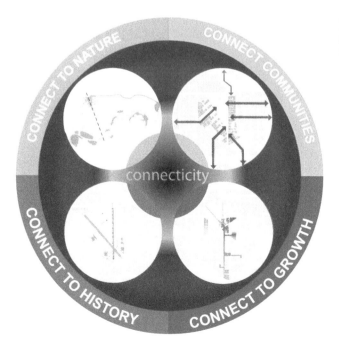

◀ Figure 8.2

Connect-i-city (courtesy BJAL and P+W Joint Venture)

as Past President of the Fort Edmonton Historical Foundation and a Board member for a decade, one major achievement is approval of a Master Development Plan to refresh the site as the largest living history museum in Canada.

In Ottawa, the same commitment involves Board membership and the Past President position of the Canadian Architectural Certification Board (CACB). This begins with (alongside several colleagues in Edmonton) the establishment of the Innovative Practice Group in Architecture (IPGA) at the former Faculty of Environmental Design, University of Calgary, providing satellite studios for the Graduate School of Architecture to deliver the Professional Practice curriculum in 'block weeks'. An Adjunct instructor for over a decade, my interest in sustainable design reaches dozens of students.

Since that time, numerous ongoing associations with Schools of Architecture across the country have been formed. I serve as a member of the Global Studio at the RAIC Centre for Architecture at Athabasca University, connecting students from around the world via lectures and a program of online mentorship.

As Chancellor of the College of Fellows of the Royal Architectural Institute of Canada (RAIC) for six years, my work champions the growth of the College to include an increase of 48% of the female membership; the founding of the online RAIC Centre for Architecture at Athabasca University, liaison with the National Gallery of Canada to secure the restoration of the Canada Pavilion in Venice, Italy for the architecture and fine arts Biennale and the building of the prestigious RAIC International Prize as a legacy project for RAIC.

My part time tenure as the Director of Practice for the Alberta Association of Architects until 2019 helps me to retain currency with my peer group and CoP. As a Director of the Arthur Erickson Foundation I help to preserve the legacy of my former employer and mentor.

The practice is recognized in an extensive survey of Canadian architecture by Elsa Lam and Graham Livesey entitled Canadian Modern Architecture, 2019.

Index

Note: Locators in *italic* indicate figures, in **bold** tables, and in ***bold italic*** boxes.

T - #0088 - 151024 - C258 - 246/174/15 [17] - CB - 9781032540252 - Matt Lamination